THE CRAFT BREWERY COOKBOOK

The Craft Brewery COOKBOOK

Recipes to Pair with Your Favorite Beers

JOHN HOLL

PHOTOGRAPHY BY JON PAGE

PRINCETON ARCHITECTURAL PRESS · NEW YORK

FOR APRIL

Published by
Princeton Architectural Press
70 West 36th Street
New York, NY 10018
www.papress.com

Editor: Holly La Due
Designers: Paul Wagner, Natalie Snodgrass

Library of Congress Cataloging-in-Publication Data
Names: Holl, John, author. | Page, Jon (Photographer), photographer.
Title: The craft brewery cookbook : recipes to pair with your favorite
    beers / by John Holl ; photography by Jon Page.
Description: New York : Princeton Architectural Press, [2022] | Includes
    index. | Summary: "Delicious and seasonal recipes and the beers to
    pair them with, from the country's best independent breweries"
    —Provided by publisher.
Identifiers: LCCN 2021029587 | ISBN 9781648960321
Subjects: LCSH: Cooking (Beer) | Cooking, American. | LCGFT: Cookbooks.
Classification: LCC TX726.3 .H66 2022 | DDC 641.6/23z—dc23
LC record available at https://lccn.loc.gov/2021029587

CONTENTS

INTRODUCTION

Beer itself is a culinary achievement.

The humble combination of water, grain, hops, and yeast is able to create familiar flavors and aromas that are rooted in our world's modern food culture, and thus make it the ideal adult beverage companion to any meal.

But that's not how everyone sees it. Because of the disruption that Prohibition caused in the history of American beer making, and the subsequent decades after its repeal, when only a handful of large breweries remained in the country—and basically all made slight variations on the same style, the bland American lager— beer has been playing catch-up with the minds and taste buds of drinkers for decades.

It's true that going back to the 1960s, advertisements from the likes of Budweiser and Coors Banquet suggested pairing lagers with the meat, potato, and vegetable dinners cooked at home, or alongside a cut of steak at a restaurant. But it was the wine industry that largely ran the table when it came to asserting itself as a steady food companion. Thanks to a price point that could denote a special occasion, and some great marketing, wine has long been what went with dinner, because that's just the way it was.

The beer industry has made extraordinary strides over the last five decades. These days, there are nearly ten thousand operating American breweries—most of them small, independently owned, and serving local communities—and they're pushing the boundaries of what beer is and can be.

Throughout the 1980s and 1990s, brewers began to experiment with ingredients, going heavy on hops to impart big citrus or pine flavors to batches of ale, as well as adding spices and specialty grains to the mix. Looking around the world for inspiration, American brewers found it in other sophisticated beer cultures, replicated it, and then quickly went to work adapting those recipes to suit their tastes and needs. Over time craft beer started showing up in restaurant kitchens where chefs were drinking the good stuff in the back and it soon appeared on menus. These beers embraced flavor, and soon enough those beers were showing up as dinner pairings on their menus.

By the 2000s the number of American breweries began to increase at a breakneck pace. Each new entrant in the space seemed committed to pushing limits, experimenting with new flavors, and trying to make up for all the years American beer was known as just fizzy, yellow lager. They drove the alcohol by volume (abv) into the double digits, packed more hops than some thought reasonable into each barrel, aged stouts on bourbon casks just to see what would happen, and found ways to incorporate just about anything that could be eaten into a beer.

It was silly at times, and still is. But there was flavor and excitement in the industry, and a generation of drinkers have since entered their twenty-first year with so much choice that it can seem overwhelming.

It has been said that brewers are like chefs because their beer recipes can be creative, unexpected, and well executed but it's more apt to compare them to bakers. Careful attention must be paid to exact ingredient measurements, proper temperature must be maintained throughout the brewing and fermentation process, and beer must be served at the peak of its freshness. It's a careful science, exacting and nuanced, as well as great creative work.

Whether you prefer the cook or baker analogy, the connection to food and food artisans is undeniable. It's difficult to find a brewer who isn't enamored with food, friends with inventive chefs, and (more than) dabbling in their own home kitchen. As brewers were experimenting with excess in their beers in the early 2000s, they were also finding foods to match. Brewpub menus from that era were filled with gourmet heart-stopping burgers, loaded everything, over-the-top tacos, and sweets that gave dentists night terrors.

Then those brewers—and we drinkers—got older. As our metabolisms slowed, we started thinking about our health a little more. While all those intense beer and food pairings and indulgent meals worked in terms of flavor, we're now more focused on moderation, healthfulness, and fresh, locally sourced ingredients.

Beer dinners became world-class meals in the 2010s. Chefs and brewers explored the nuances of what was in the glass and how it complemented or contrasted with what was on the plate. They also dialed back the excess. Gluttonous and heavily caloric meals were replaced with lighter options, and brewers who once embraced high-alcohol offerings tried formulating styles to register at 100 calories or fewer while retaining flavor.

Today, for the adventurous, beer has even come to emulate food. Some brewers mimic the flavors of candies and pastries, add whole chickens to the mash, or make beers that taste more like hot sauce than actual ale. There are many gimmick beers out there, but more often brewers are using natural ingredients in ways that tease out new flavors. Brewers have become friends with farmers and are adding fresh fruits and vegetables to classic recipes that offer lovely aromas that are reminiscent of being in an orchard. Hop farmers are also pushing innovation and creating new varieties that evoke the scent of tropical fruits and herbs, or wood and berries. With so much on offer, it's easy to get lost in the aromas and flavors. Even though these fine beers easily stand alone, when paired with the right dish the whole experience is elevated.

There's a nonsense expression that has been used with wine for years: Red wine goes with red meat, and white wine goes with chicken or fish. This is largely useless advice and tells a diner nothing about either the specifics of the beverage or the meal itself. Still, the catchphrase has stuck with people over the decades. There is no such quick phrase when it comes to beer and food pairings. Beer is too varied, too complex, too flavorful to be boxed in. So, it is up to the chef and brewer to find connections between their creations that speak well with each other.

To find these connections, it helps to take a closer look at the beverage itself. The four main ingredients in beer are water, grain, hops, and yeast. Layered on top of those is an endless buffet of ingredients that intrepid brewers are adding to recipes. When considering the core four individually, it becomes clear how each brings important (and familiar) food flavors to your pint. Pair that pint with the right dish, however, and you've created a culinary experience that is a sensory delight.

Let's start with water, which can be soft or hard, or have varying degrees of salinity. There's also certainly a difference between treated city water and water drawn from a cool country well. It can also be neutral, like water from a bottle.

Next, grains, which are typically kilned or roasted before being added to beer and are primarily malt, wheat, oats, and rye. Malt can have a slight toasted aspect, like Cheerios, or it can be darker and take on flavors of Grape Nuts, actual toast, caramel, chocolate, coffee, or toffee. It can even be burnt acrid black. If that sounds weird, think about going to a brick oven pizzeria. When the fresh pie hits the table, the dough bubbles that had risen on the crust and expanded have burst into carbon ash. That nub is what most people reach for, even though the flavor isn't as appealing as, say, mozzarella or garlic. There are even malts dried over open flames, imparting a smoky flavor. Wheat can add a fullness like bread to beer, while rye brings a spicy character to a recipe.

Hops are the problematic ingredient. They are part of the cannabis family, but you can't do with hops what you do with marijuana. Seriously, don't try. Hops are good for one thing only: making beer. And here's where the trouble comes in. Despite being used to bring aroma and flavor to beer for countless generations, they've long been associated with a single flavor—bitterness. Learning to either taste past that, or better yet to embrace it, opens the taste buds to better experiences. Hops can smell or taste like citrus, strawberries, pine, and so much more. Two of the most popular hop varieties today are Citra and Mosaic, which impart flavors of orange, lime, pineapple, mango, and passion fruit.

And finally, there is yeast. It is the most important ingredient, as it's the microbe that converts sugar in unfermented beer into alcohol, and depending on the strain, it can bring flavors and aromas of honey, flowers, bubble gum, banana, clove, spice, leather, tobacco, and more.

This book is a collection of recipes from small breweries throughout the country. Grouped by beer style, its aim is to help unlock some of the connections that exist between the glass and the plate. The chefs and brewers who shared their recipes are not only talking about flavors but also conveying a sense of place.

Beer is a locally made product. It is possible for the majority of Americans to walk into a local brewery, see the equipment and the raw ingredients, and meet the brewers. Buying beer from these breweries supports not just the brewery but other small local businesses, as brewers will often add ingredients like fruit, vegetables, and herbs that come from local farms. Others have fun and will add regional sweets to the mash for pastry stouts or sours. These beers offer a taste of home and hometown pride and can offer greater insight into a town, city, region, or state for outside drinkers.

The pairings in this book also highlight where they come from, featuring seafood from New England and the West Coast, hearty meat dishes from the Midwest, and vegetables from agricultural regions across the country. And just as chefs like to cook with local ingredients, you can too. When planning out a meal look for local vendors and producers for meats, honey, vegetables, fish, and nuts. It adds not only flavor but satisfaction to a meal knowing the local food economy has benefited.

You can build a multicourse beer dinner from this book with different styles and flavors, and along the way you might find some unexpected synergy. The at-home beer and food experience is an adventure in which you are in control and experimentation is encouraged. Finding a great pairing can start with a particular ingredient, a whole dish, or a beer itself—it's about bringing them together in harmony.

Since the arrival of microbreweries, beer in the United States has been on an upward trajectory both in consumer sales and the number of breweries operating in our hometowns. With so much beer choice available from our breweries, and chefs championing local and innovative flavors, there has never been a better time for a proper beer dinner.

Glassware and Service

What is the best style of glass for beer? There are countless ways to answer that question. While there are glasses designed for specific beers like Kölsch, for everyday home use, a short-stemmed tulip glass is the best overall option. Just avoid a standard pint glass. They're functional but offer no real benefit to the beer itself.

Whatever type of glass you serve beer in, it should be a clean glass. It is best to use your beer glasses for just beer and to wash them by hand, avoiding harsh chemical soaps that can leave residue, and allowing them to air dry. Rinsing the inside of your glass with cold water before serving is also recommended to wash away any dust or debris. If you pour beer into a glass and see carbonation sticking to the walls, that means there's residue left behind. In the same way you wouldn't accept a dirty fork at a restaurant, make sure your glassware is clean and ready.

Properly pouring beer into a glass benefits not only its appearance but also its aroma. Tilt the glass in one hand and quickly pour the contents of the can or bottle down its side until the liquid reaches about the halfway mark. Then straighten the glass and continue a fast pour to help create a head of foam. Using a slightly larger glass than the amount of beer allows for proper foam to form and aromatics to be released.

Lager and Pilsner

Lager and pilsner are the most popular beer styles in the world. Built on the backs of the world's largest brewing companies, including Heineken and Anheuser-Busch InBev, today's lagers and pilsners are crisp, clean, and generally well balanced between malt and hop flavors. They can also be described by some beer lovers as bland and soulless. While not completely fair, comparing them to Wonder Bread is not too far off, especially in a world where artisanal bakers are producing such flavorful loaves.

Thankfully, over the last few years, craft brewers have developed a renewed interest in lagers and pilsners, bringing new dimensions to the category. This resurgence is happening for several reasons: Craft brewers in America now have the bandwidth, talent, and ability to make lagers, alongside the ales that have so long been their preferred category. Plus, drinkers want small-batch beer that's snappy, refreshing, and flavorful, and that celebrates the four core ingredients. Lagers are humble but very hard to make. Often middle-of-the-road alcohol by volume content (abv), they are built for session drinking and the really good ones start to get interesting after the third pint.

Renewed consumer interest means that some brewers are branching out beyond the well-known light pilsners and lagers of days past and bringing back styles like Schwarzbier that have been sidelined for too long. Still, most breweries are sticking to tradition, making uncomplicated Czech- or German-style lagers with noble hops that offer spicy or earthy notes, and clean yeast that leaves a crisp finish. Some are adding healthy doses of new-world hops, with tropical fruit aromas, or leaving their lagers and pilsners unfiltered for a hazy look that is popular with IPAs these days.

Dark lagers are also experiencing a bit of a resurgence thanks to higher-roasted malts that lend an appealing depth to their flavors. In this instance, dark does not equal roasted flavor like in a stout or porter but is more akin to the notes found in toffee, stewed fruits, and roasted nuts.

Because of their malt-forward flavors, dark lagers are most often referred to as "liquid bread" and styles like a Dunkel or Doppelbock have flavors and aromas reminiscent of the crust of baked bread. A higher abv also helps add body and heft.

Lagers and pilsners are workhorses in the kitchen. Given their clean flavors, you can pour a glass and serve it alongside just about anything from rich meats to sweets and have an enjoyable experience. But look for earthy or herbal flavors from your foods, or light and fresh ingredients. In other cases, a refreshing lager can help balance oil and fats or keep acidity in check. They can also quench saltiness and increase spice intensity.

For quick pairings, look to a lager's country of origin. Flavors develop over time and work in tandem, so dishes and flavors popular through Europe will work with European pilsners. Hearty dishes from the heartland of America will be complemented by light lagers, often brewed with corn or rice.

Thanks to their ubiquitous nature, lagers are usually a drinker's first experience with beer. If served warm or at a bad college party, their overall lack of sweetness helps put a lot of people off drinking beer all together. Pairing lagers with food can bring them back. The right dish helps reveal the nuance of flavors in the glass. Give these pairings a try and find some lager love.

TACOS DE PAPA

Serves 6 to 8

FILLING

1½ lbs russet potatoes, peeled and cubed
4 garlic cloves, peeled and minced
Fine sea salt

SALSA

5 dried guajillo chiles, stemmed and seeded, plus additional as needed
8 tomatillos, plus additional as needed
2 bay leaves
2 cloves
4 garlic cloves, peeled
Fine sea salt
1 white onion, diced (optional)
Chopped fresh cilantro (optional)

TACOS

3 Tbsp vegetable oil
12 to 14 corn tortillas (OK to substitute flour)
1 cup shredded cabbage (optional)
8 oz crema fresca (optional)
8 oz Cotija (optional)

Heirloom Rustic Ales

TULSA, OKLAHOMA

The Pairing: Mexican Lager

Tacos and lager are always a good decision and a great pairing. These vegetarian tacos from Chef Chris Castro rely on potatoes for heft and have a good amount of spice and even a little acidity. The lager should showcase a biscuity malt and low earthy hops, which help keep the vegetables grounded and the spice in balance.

To make the filling: In a large pot, cover the potatoes and garlic with water, and bring to a boil over high heat. Once the water is boiling, lower the heat to medium-low and simmer for 15 minutes, or until the potatoes are soft and can be easily pierced by a fork. Drain the potatoes and garlic, transfer to a large bowl, and mash or use a ricer to fully combine and season with salt.

Meanwhile, make the salsa: In a dry pan over medium-low heat, lightly toast the chiles for about 4 minutes, or until fragrant. Remove from heat and set aside.

Remove the husks from the tomatillos and rinse off any sticky residue.

Fill a small saucepan a quarter of the way with water and add 3 of the toasted chiles, 4 of the tomatillos, the bay leaves, and the cloves. Bring to a boil over medium heat then lower the heat to low and simmer for about 10 to 12 minutes, or until the tomatillos turn yellowish. Strain, reserving both the solids and the liquid.

In a molcajete (lava rock mortar and pestle) or in a blender or food processor, mash or blend the garlic and salt into a paste. Add the cooked tomatillo mixture, along with the remaining 2 toasted chiles, and mash or blend them into the garlic paste.

Dice the remaining 4 tomatillos, add to the garlic paste, and mash or blend into a chunky paste. Taste the salsa: If it's too tart, add another chile, and if it's too spicy, add more tomatillos. If the salsa is too thick, gradually add splashes of the reserved tomatillo cooking water until the desired thickness is achieved. Add onion and cilantro (if using). Refrigerate until ready to serve.

Heirloom Rustic Ales
The name might be misleading, as this brewery in Tulsa is quickly becoming known for its lagers. Jake Miller, the brewer and owner, has committed the brewery to creating fresh, flavorful lagers and ales that honor tradition, and are meant to be accompaniments to conversation, while also stimulating the taste buds.

To make the tacos: In a large skillet over medium heat, heat the vegetable oil. Put 3 or 4 tortillas in the skillet, add ¼ cup of the mashed potatoes to each, and let cook for 2 minutes, or until the tortillas are warm. Carefully fold the tortillas over and cook for 3 to 4 minutes per side, or until crispy and golden brown. Repeat with the remaining tortillas and mashed potatoes. Serve immediately with shredded cabbage, crema, Cotija, and the salsa.

A.B.L.T. SALAD

Serves 4 to 6

BACON
4 cups light or dark
   brown sugar
1 tsp cayenne pepper
1 lb bacon

CRACKERS
3 cups all-purpose flour
1 Tbsp freshly ground
   black pepper
¾ tsp fine sea salt
⅓ cup olive oil

VINAIGRETTE
1 cup smoked or traditional
   tomato purée
1 cup red wine vinegar
½ cup Dijon mustard
¼ cup light or dark
   brown sugar
¼ cup canola oil
Fine sea salt and freshly
   ground black pepper

SALAD
4 cups baby arugula and
   mixed salad greens
2 avocados, thinly sliced
1 medium red onion,
   finely diced

Chuckanut Brewery and Kitchen
BURLINGTON, WASHINGTON

The Pairing: Light Lager

Spelling it all the way out, this salad is an indulgent combination of creamy avocado, candied bacon, peppered lavash crackers, and smoked tomato vinaigrette. This dish is a signature at the Chuckanut Pub, created by Chef Ben Fulks. Now, I won't tell you how to run your kitchen, but the candied bacon is so good that snacky hands might eat it all before it gets combined with the rest of the dish, so making extra is advised.

To make the candied bacon: Preheat the oven to 300°F. Line a baking sheet with parchment paper.

In a large bowl, mix together the brown sugar and cayenne until fully combined. Rub each slice of bacon in the sugar mixture then transfer to the prepared baking sheet. Bake for 30 to 40 minutes, or until the fat is rendered and the bacon is covered in a caramel-like coating. Set aside to cool then break into pieces.

Meanwhile, make the cracker dough: In a large bowl, combine the flour, pepper, salt, 1 cup of warm water, and olive oil and knead until a smooth dough forms. Divide the dough into three equal pieces and wrap each piece in plastic wrap. Allow to rest for at least 30 minutes at room temperature.

Meanwhile, make the vinaigrette: In a medium bowl, combine the smoked tomato purée, red wine vinegar, Dijon mustard, and brown sugar. Using an immersion blender (or a standard blender), blend until smooth and fully incorporated. With the blender on, gradually add the canola oil, increasing the flow of the oil as you incorporate it. Season with salt and pepper. The vinaigrette can be refrigerated in an airtight container for up 2 weeks.

To bake the crackers: Preheat the oven to 425°F. Line a baking sheet with parchment paper.

Working with one piece of dough at a time, on a lightly floured surface, roll the dough as thin as possible and transfer to prepared baking sheet, filling the sheet. Bake for about 20 minutes, or until golden brown. Allow to cool then break the cracker into large pieces. Repeat with the remaining dough.

To make the salad: Toss the arugula and salad greens with a desired amount of the vinaigrette then top with the candied bacon, crackers, avocado, and red onion. Serve immediately.

> ### *Chuckanut Brewery and Kitchen*
> *This brewery has been making craft lagers long before it was considered cool. Headed by brewing royalty Mari and Will Kemper, Chuckanut currently operates two locations: a large brewery and tap room in Burlington, Washington, near the Canadian border, and a taproom in Portland, Oregon. How beloved is this brewery? Mention the name to beer professionals or drinkers in the know and an instant smile will cross their faces.*

HOUSE LAGER MUSSELS WITH ZHOUG

Jack's Abby Craft Lagers

FRAMINGHAM, MASSACHUSETTS

The Pairing: Helles

Beer and mussels are a classic pairing, and cooking the shellfish in a beer-infused broth adds to the experience. Any lighter colored and flavored style will do, but Helles works best as both an ingredient and pairing. The soft and bready malt character of this German-style lager makes it a terrific complement to shellfish. Its sweetness is balanced by the spiciness of the zhoug—a Middle Eastern condiment, similar to pesto but with some hot pepper heat—while its slight carbonation helps cool down your palate from the bite of the jalapeño. Lemon, both in the zhoug and served alongside, imparts brightness that brings out the citrus in the hops. Delicious seafood, crunchy bread, and award-winning beer—you can't go wrong.

Serves 2 to 4

ZHOUG

2 whole jalapeños, stemmed
2 garlic cloves, peeled
1 bunch fresh cilantro leaves, chopped
1 tsp ground cumin
½ tsp ground cardamom
½ tsp Aleppo chile flakes
½ tsp fine sea salt
½ cup extra-virgin olive oil, plus more as needed
2 Tbsp lemon juice

MUSSELS

2 Tbsp canola oil
1½ lbs mussels, washed and scrubbed
1 cup Helles lager
4 Tbsp (½ stick) unsalted butter
1 tsp garlic paste
Fine sea salt and freshly ground black pepper
½ tsp red pepper flakes
2 Tbsp sliced scallions
½ lemon, grilled
Sourdough toast, for serving

To make the zhoug: In a food processor, combine the jalapeños, garlic, cilantro, cumin, cardamom, chile flakes, salt, olive oil, and lemon juice. Blend until fully combined, adding more oil as needed if a thinner consistency is desired. Set aside. The zhoug can be refrigerated in an airtight container for up to 4 days.

To make the mussels: In a large sauté pan or Dutch oven, heat the canola oil over high heat until shimmering. Add the mussels and sauté, stirring often, for 2 minutes. Add the lager, butter, and garlic paste then season with salt and pepper and stir to combine. Cover and cook for about 5 minutes, or until the mussels have opened. Add the zhoug and sauté for about 4 minutes, or until aromatic. Remove from the heat, discard any mussels that have not opened, and add the red pepper flakes. Transfer the mussels and broth to a serving bowl, sprinkle with scallions, and serve with grilled lemon and sourdough toast.

Jack's Abby Craft Lagers

Three brothers helm this lager-focused brewery, but it's actually named after one of their wives. That would be Abby, Jack Hendler's wife. The brewery name is also a nod to the monastic brewing tradition, but lest you think it revolves around the more familiar Belgian tradition, here the focus is German monastic brewing. Those were the breweries responsible for introducing lagers to the world, promoting the use of hops, and standardizing brewing procedures. Today, this brewery is leading the American craft lager conversation.

DEVILED EGGS

Serves 4 to 6

12 large eggs
¼ cup mayonnaise
¼ cup sour cream
1 Tbsp minced shallots
1 tsp minced fresh chives
1 tsp minced fresh tarragon
1 tsp minced fresh
   flat-leaf parsley
1 tsp paprika
½ tsp cayenne pepper
Lemon juice
Kosher salt
2 cornichons, sliced

Rockwell Beer Company
ST. LOUIS, MISSOURI

The Pairing: Bohemian Pilsner

Brothers Jonathan and Brian Moxey contributed this recipe. "Deviled eggs have always been a part of our family gatherings and turns out they're also one of my favorite beer-drinking foods," says Jonathan, the brewer at Rockwell Beer Company. "I love the way that pilsner complements the herbs and acidity of the filling while cutting through the fat. The carbonation washes it all clean and gets you ready for the next egg." To give the eggs a Caesar salad–inspired twist, see the note at the bottom of the recipe.

In a large pot, bring 4 quarts of water to a boil. Fill a large bowl with ice and cold water.

Carefully lower the eggs into the boiling water and cook for 12 minutes. Using a slotted spoon, transfer the eggs from the boiling water to the bowl of ice water. Let the eggs chill until cool enough to handle then gently crack and peel. Cut the eggs lengthwise in half then remove the yolks and transfer to a food processor; set the whites aside.

Add the mayo and sour cream to the food processor and purée until smooth. Transfer the mixture to a medium bowl and fold in the shallots, chives, tarragon, and parsley. Transfer the mixture to a disposable pastry bag or a resealable plastic bag and cut the end of the pastry bag or the corner of the plastic bag so there is a roughly ¼ to ½ in opening.

Dust the cut sides of the egg whites with paprika and cayenne then pipe the egg yolk mixture into the center of each one. Season with lemon juice and salt, top with a sliver of cornichon, and serve. These may also be made up to a day ahead of time.

Note: To make Caesar Salad Deviled Eggs (pictured opposite), replace the shallot and herbs with 2 minced brown anchovy fillets, the zest of 1 lemon, and 2 finely chopped romaine lettuce leaves. Skip the paprika and cayenne and lay a ribbon of romaine over the egg white before filling. Top with freshly grated Parmesan cheese and freshly ground black pepper.

Rockwell Beer Company

A healthy respect for tradition combined with a desire to find and incorporate new flavors into beer has established Rockwell Beer Co. as a new generation leader in the well-established St. Louis craft beer scene. From beers like the Stand By, a hoppy pilsner, to the brewery's robust mixed fermentation program, Rockwell has a beer for every palate.

BREAKFAST BURRITO WITH NEW MEXICAN RED CHILE SAUCE

Serves 4 to 6

CHILE SAUCE

6 oz dried New Mexican
    red chiles or ancho or
    Anaheim chiles
3 Tbsp lard or vegetable oil
1 medium white onion,
    chopped
12 garlic cloves, minced
1 Tbsp ground cumin
1½ tsp dried oregano
1 Tbsp plus 1 tsp sherry
    vinegar
1 Tbsp kosher salt
1 tsp granulated sugar

BURRITOS

1 lb chorizo sausage,
    finely chopped
1 lb frozen tater tots
8 large eggs
¼ cup whole milk
2 Tbsp unsalted butter
Fine sea salt and freshly
    ground black pepper
½ cup shredded Cheddar
    cheese or Gouda
Four 10 in flour tortillas

Bierstadt Lagerhaus

DENVER, COLORADO

The Pairing: Dunkel

Cofounder and head brewer of Bierstadt Lagerhaus Ashleigh Carter, who has family roots in New Mexico, enhances her hearty red chile sauce with the slightly sweet and roasted undertones of a Dunkel. You can make the chile sauce in advance, so the flavors have time to mingle, and then serve it atop a breakfast burrito. It also goes great with enchiladas or braised pork, as a base for meat or vegetable chilis, or just about anything else you can imagine. Breakfast burritos are holy in beer and brewery circles. Hearty and filling, they're a perfect meal to start off a long day at work (or play) or to help ease the pain of a long night of work (or play). Be generous with the sauce—no one will fault you for using a knife and fork for this typically handheld food.

To make the chile sauce: Rinse the chiles, split them open, and discard the stems and seeds. Put the chiles in a large heatproof bowl. Bring 8 cups of water to a boil and pour over the chiles. Cover the bowl and soak the chiles, stirring occasionally, for about 30 minutes or until softened. Strain and reserve the chiles and the liquid.

In a large, heavy saucepan, heat the lard over medium-low heat. Add the onion, garlic, cumin, and oregano and cook for about 6 minutes or until the onion is soft. Transfer to a blender, add the softened chiles, and purée, adding splashes of the chile soaking liquid as needed to help blend the mixture, until smooth (use caution when blending hot liquids). Pour through a fine-mesh strainer set over a bowl and use a spatula to press as much liquid out of the mixture as possible; discard any solids.

Return the mixture to the same large, heavy saucepan and simmer, partially covered and whisking occasionally, for about 30 minutes, or until thickened. Add the vinegar, salt, and sugar. Taste the sauce and season with more vinegar, salt, and sugar as needed. The chile sauce can be refrigerated in an airtight container overnight.

To make the burritos: In a large skillet over medium-high heat, cook the chorizo, stirring often, for about 10 minutes, or until the fat has rendered and the sausage is browned and crispy on the edges. Transfer the sausage to a paper towel–lined plate to drain. Add the tater tots to the pan, place over medium-high heat, and cook in the sausage fat for

Bierstadt Lagerhaus

Good things take time. The Bierstadt Lagerhaus is a dream turned reality by longtime brewers Ashleigh Carter and Bill Eye, who transformed a downtown Denver warehouse into a temple of lager. It's only lagers and pilsners on the beer menu, brewed according to tradition on a reclaimed German brewhouse and aged for weeks before serving. Their signature, the Slow Pour Pils, takes five minutes to get from tap to glass to table. It is always worth the wait.

7 to 10 minutes, or until warmed through and crispy. Transfer the tater tots to a cutting board and finely chop. Return the tater tots to the pan and cook over medium-high heat, for about 3 minutes, or until lightly golden all over. Transfer the tater tots to a bowl and add the chorizo.

In a medium bowl, whisk together the eggs and milk.

In a large skillet, melt the butter over medium heat. Add the egg mixture and cook, stirring frequently to scramble, for 4 minutes or until the desired level of doneness for the curds is achieved. Season with salt and pepper, add the cheese, and toss to combine. Add the egg mixture to the chorizo and tater tots and stir to fully combine. Keep warm.

Wipe the skillet clean and place over low heat. Warm the tortillas, one at a time, for about 30 seconds per side, or until soft and warmed through. Place the tortillas on plates and scoop the egg and chorizo mixture into the middle of each. Fold in the sides and roll up each tortilla to form burritos. Top with chile sauce and serve immediately.

HOMINY CORN POSOLE

Serves 4 to 6

HOMINY

1 cup dried hominy corn
  (posole), white, blue,
  or a combination

STEW

1 Tbsp sunflower oil
1 large onion, chopped
12 garlic cloves, minced
1 to 2 dried New Mexican
  red chiles or ancho or
  Anaheim chiles, seeded,
  stemmed, and crumbled
2 Tbsp mild red New Mexican
  chile powder, or similar
1 Tbsp azafrán (Native
  American saffron)
½ tsp dried Mexican oregano
  or hand-harvested wild
  Sonoran oregano
¼ tsp dried thyme
1 tsp fine sea salt
6 sprigs fresh cilantro or
  flat-leaf parsley
6 lime wedges, for serving
Warm bread, for serving
  (optional)

Bow and Arrow Brewing Co.
ALBUQUERQUE, NEW MEXICO

The Pairing: Corn Pilsner

Posole is a simple, rustic hominy stew common throughout many Native American communities and made in a variety of different ways. The word *posole* is Spanish for hominy, which is usually sold dried in the Latino food section of grocery stores or at farmer's markets, as well as frozen. While the canned version is an option, it never tastes quite right. Chef Lois Ellen Frank of Red Mesa Cuisine in Santa Fe—a catering and food company serving Native American dishes with a contemporary twist—says this is one of her favorite versions of the stew, as it really features just the posole but it can be served with wild game or other proteins. This recipe requires overnight preparation.

To make the hominy: Soak the dried hominy in 1 qt of water overnight.

The following day, drain the hominy and discard the water. Put the hominy in a large pot and add about 8 cups of water—add more water as needed to cover the hominy by at least 3 in. Bring to a boil over high heat then turn the heat to low and simmer, uncovered, adding water as needed to keep the hominy covered by 3 in, for about 2 hours, or until the kernels burst and are puffy and tender—white hominy tends to puff the most.

Strain the hominy, reserving both the hominy and the water—you should have 3 to 4 cups of water.

To make the stew: In a 6 qt pot, heat the sunflower oil over medium-high heat. Add the onion and sauté for 2 to 3 minutes, or until translucent. Add the garlic and sauté for 3 to 5 minutes, or until fragrant. Add the crumbled red chiles, chile powder, and azafrán then stir and cook for another 3 minutes, or until starting to brown. Add the cooked hominy, along with 4 cups of the reserved hominy cooking water, and bring to a boil then turn the heat to low and simmer for about 15 minutes to bring the flavors together. Add the oregano, thyme, and salt, and cook for an additional 5 minutes.

Serve hot with cilantro or parsley, lime wedges, and warm bread (if using).

Bow and Arrow Brewing Co.

When Shyla Sheppard and Missy Begay started Bow and Arrow, they wanted their beers to honor the local area as well as their heritage. They make traditional IPAs and sours, of course, but also ales made with Navajo tea and pilsners made with blue corn and any number of spices native to the Southwest. A brewery proud of its lineage and eager to share Native American history while keeping traditions alive, Bow and Arrow is one to seek out.

MUSHROOM AND ROOT VEGETABLE BISCUIT POT PIE

Serves 6

BISCUITS

2 cups all-purpose flour
½ cup whole wheat flour
1¾ tsp baking powder
1½ tsp fine sea salt
1 tsp freshly ground
black pepper
1 tsp granulated sugar
½ tsp baking soda
½ cup (1 stick) plus 2 Tbsp
cold unsalted butter,
cubed, plus 1 Tbsp for
brushing
1 cup sour cream
⅓ cup whole milk

continues →

Heater Allen Brewing

MCMINNVILLE, OREGON

The Pairing: Schwarzbier

A full Dutch oven simmering on the stove is a wonderful aromatic pleasure at home in the warmer months. Using simple ingredients, this hearty vegetarian option can come together quickly on a weeknight or work as a weekend meal. Leftovers are especially good after the flavors have time to mingle.

To make the biscuit dough: Preheat the oven to 425°F.

In a large bowl, whisk together the all-purpose and whole wheat flours, baking powder, salt, pepper, sugar, and baking soda. Add the butter and use your hands to mix it into the dry ingredients, coating the butter and flattening all of the cubes, until the mixture looks crumbly.

Create a well in the center, add the sour cream, and use a fork or spoon to stir it into the flour mixture. Once the sour cream is mostly blended in, add the milk, and stir to moisten any remaining dry bits left in the dough. A few dry bits are ok, but if there are a lot, gradually add 2 to 4 tablespoons of milk.

On a lightly floured surface, shape the dough into a rough rectangle. Fold the sides inward, press down, and shape into another rough rectangle. Repeat the process two more times for a total of three folds. Shape the dough into a rectangle one more time, wrap in plastic wrap, and refrigerate while you cook the filling.

Heater Allen Brewing

In the hop-forward landscape that is Oregon brewing, Heater Allen's lagers stand out for their thoughtfulness, attention to detail, and refreshing nature. These days, it's a family affair with Lisa Allen running the brewery her father Rick started in 2007—Rick's is the classic story of a home brewer who went pro and decided to make the beers he wanted to drink. Although she was fascinated by fermentation and brewing science from a young age, Lisa didn't plan on joining her father's business and instead went into wine making. But, as fate would have it, Lisa eventually started helping at the brewhouse a dozen years ago and hasn't left. It's been to the great benefit of us all.

FILLING

2 Tbsp unsalted butter

1 lb cremini mushrooms, stemmed and thinly sliced

Fine sea salt and freshly ground black pepper

1 large onion, diced

4 garlic cloves, minced

2 tsp finely chopped fresh rosemary

2 tsp finely chopped thyme

1 medium to large parsnip, peeled and diced

2 medium carrots, peeled and diced

3 Tbsp all-purpose flour, plus more as needed

2 cups mushroom or vegetable broth

1 Tbsp fish sauce (optional)

To make the filling: In a large Dutch oven or other heavy ovenproof pot, melt 1 Tbsp of the butter over medium-high heat. Add the mushrooms, season generously with salt and pepper, and cook for 5 to 8 minutes, or until the mushrooms are soft and release some of their liquid. Using a slotted spoon, transfer the mushrooms to a plate and set aside. Add the remaining 1 Tbsp of butter to the mushroom liquid in the pot and melt over medium-high heat. Add the onion and garlic and cook for 1 minute then add the rosemary and thyme and cook for 1 minute. Add the parsnip and cook for about 5 minutes, or until soft but still firm. Add the carrots, season with salt and pepper, and cook for another 5 minutes. Return the mushrooms to the pot, sprinkle with the flour, and stir to coat the vegetables. Add the broth and cook for about 15 minutes, or until thick. (If the broth doesn't thicken after 5 minutes, add another 1 Tbsp of flour.) Add the fish sauce (if using).

Remove the biscuit dough from the refrigerator and cut the rectangle into six equal pieces. Place the biscuits evenly on top of the filling, leaving a small amount of space between each one.

Melt the remaining 1 Tbsp of butter and lightly brush the top of the biscuits for a bit of extra browning. Put the Dutch oven uncovered into the oven for 15 to 20 minutes or until the top of the biscuits are golden and the filling is bubbling. Let sit 5 minutes before serving.

JÄGER-SCHNITZEL

Serves 4

½ lb bacon, diced

4 boneless pork loin chops or veal chops, pounded to ¼ in thickness

1 tsp fine salt

1 tsp freshly ground black pepper

½ cup all-purpose flour

1 tsp garlic powder

1 tsp paprika

2 large eggs, lightly beaten

¾ cup breadcrumbs

4 Tbsp unsalted butter or canola oil, for frying

MUSHROOM GRAVY (MAKES 2 CUPS)

2 Tbsp bacon grease (from the Jägerschnitzel)

1 medium yellow onion, chopped

1 garlic clove, minced

1 lb cremini mushrooms, sliced

4 Tbsp (½ stick) unsalted butter

¼ cup all-purpose flour

2 cups beef broth

1 cup Dunkel

2 tsp balsamic vinegar

¼ tsp dried thyme

2 sprigs fresh rosemary

Fine sea salt and freshly ground black pepper

Enegren Brewing Company

MOORPARK, CALIFORNIA

The Pairing: Dunkel

A staple of German cuisine, this dish can be made with either pork or veal but should always be paired with a proper mug of Dunkel. The dark lager, with its flavors of caramel and bread crust, makes a wonderful companion to the rich, savory, and earthy flavors of the dish. Jägerschnitzel can be served with spaetzle and red cabbage to enhance the experience. Top with mushroom gravy.

In a medium frying pan, cook the bacon over medium heat for about 6 minutes, or until crispy. Transfer the bacon to a paper towel–lined plate to drain and set aside to cool. Reserve 2 Tbsp of the bacon grease to make the Mushroom Gravy.

Season the pork chops with salt and pepper.

In a shallow dish combine the flour, garlic powder, and paprika. Place the eggs in a second shallow dish and put the breadcrumbs in a third shallow dish.

Dip the pork chops in the flour mixture, followed by the egg and then the breadcrumbs, coating both sides and all edges at each stage. Be careful not to press the breadcrumbs into the meat and gently shake off the excess crumbs.

In a large skillet, heat 1 Tbsp of butter or oil over medium heat.

Working in batches, put the breaded pork chops in the hot pan and fry, flipping once, for 2 to 3 minutes per side, or until golden brown all over.

Enegren Brewing Company

For more than a decade, the Southern California coast has been home to some of the country's best German-inspired lagers. Brothers Chris and Matt Enegren and friend Joe Nascenzi founded Enegren, which makes traditional styles that are both stunning and simple in their execution. While fads come and go in the beer world, Enegren's laser-like focus on lagers has served them well and gained them loyal fans across the country. They make beers for drinking with friends and family, for toasting after an honest day's work, or for simply relaxing with on a weekend.

Add more butter or oil as needed to continue frying. Transfer to a paper towel-lined plate to drain.

To make the mushroom gravy: In a large Dutch oven or other heavy pot, heat the bacon grease over medium heat. Add the onion and cook for about 5 minutes, or until translucent. Add the garlic and cook for 1 minute. Add the mushrooms and cook for about 5 minutes, or until they release their juices. Add the butter and allow to melt then gradually add the flour, stirring to coat all the ingredients. Continue cooking, stirring continuously, for about 2 minutes. Add the beef broth, beer, vinegar, and thyme, whisking continuously to combine. Season with salt and pepper and cook, whisking continuously, for about 2 to 3 minutes, or until the gravy thickens. Add the rosemary, turn the heat to low, cover, and simmer for 5 to 10 minutes. If you want a richer gravy, continue simmering to reduce. For thinner gravy add more beer and beef broth.

Cover the schnitzel with the mushroom gravy, top with bacon, and serve.

FISH AND CHIPS

Serves 4 to 6

½ cup plus 2 Tbsp all-
    purpose flour
½ cup cornstarch
1 Tbsp paprika
2 tsp fine sea salt
1 tsp baking powder
¾ cup Helles lager
2 lbs russet potatoes, washed,
    peeled, and cut into ½ in
    thick strips
1 tsp granulated sugar
4 cups vegetable oil or lard
4 thick white fish fillets such
    as halibut or cod (about
    2 lbs total), cut into
    1 in wide strips
Freshly ground black pepper
Tartar sauce or ketchup,
    for serving

Wibby Brewing
LONGMONT, COLORADO

The Pairing: Vienna Lager

A pub staple, this recipe even tastes better at home, where you can eat it hot and chase each bite with a sip of a caramel-forward but still crisp Vienna lager. This is a Wibby family recipe, shared by brewer Ryan Wibby, who makes one of the best Vienna lagers in the country. For a more authentic experience, serve your fish and chips in a basket lined with newspaper.

In a large bowl, whisk together ½ cup of the flour, the cornstarch, the paprika, 1 tsp of the salt, and the baking powder. Add the beer and whisk until smooth. Cover and refrigerate until ready to use.

In a colander, rinse the potato strips under cold running water. Transfer the potatoes to a large pot and cover with fresh cold water. Add the sugar and the remaining 1 tsp of salt and bring to a gentle boil. Turn the heat to medium and simmer for 4 minutes, or until they begin to soften. Remove from the heat, drain the potatoes, and gently pat them dry with a paper towel.

Fill a large Dutch oven, deep pot, or deep fryer with about 3 in of vegetable oil and heat to 350°F on a thermometer. Line a baking sheet with paper towels. Working in small batches, carefully add the potatoes to the hot oil and fry for 2 minutes, or until starting to turn golden. Transfer the potatoes to the paper towel–lined baking sheet and set aside. Fry the remaining potatoes, adjusting the heat as needed to keep the oil at 350°F. Keep the oil at 350°F to fry the fish.

Preheat the oven to 200°F. Arrange a wire rack on a baking sheet and put it inside the oven. Line a plate with paper towels.

Wibby Brewing
Ryan Wibby has a passion for traditional lagers but also likes to play around in the beer space. Since launching Wibby Brewing, he's racked up medals, awards, and some top-notch reviews. Like so many small brewers these days, he has worries, but he's also excited about the future and always looking for new ways to reach customers. From making lagers with cacao nibs to crafting shandies and seltzers, it's clear he's a brewer who is enjoying his days and grateful for the customers downing the pints.

Season the fish with salt and pepper. Place the remaining 2 Tbsp of flour on a plate and dredge the fish, making sure to cover all sides. Dip the fish in the batter, making sure the pieces are well coated.

Working in small batches, carefully add the fish to the hot oil and fry for about 8 minutes, or until golden brown. Transfer the fish to the paper towel-lined plate and sprinkle with salt. Transfer the fried fish to the wire rack in oven to keep warm while you fry the rest of the fish.

Turn the heat up and bring the oil temperature to 400°F. Line a baking sheet with paper towels. Working in small batches, fry the potatoes a second time for about 5 minutes, or until golden brown. Transfer the potatoes to the paper towel-lined baking sheet. Fry the remaining potatoes and serve immediately with the fish. Use tartar sauce or ketchup for dipping.

WHIPPED RICOTTA WITH HONEY, THYME, AND TOASTED CIABATTA

Serves 4

12 oz whole milk ricotta
2 Tbsp heavy cream
2 tsp fine sea salt
2 tsp freshly ground white pepper
1 cup olive oil
4 garlic cloves
12 sprigs fresh thyme
Zest of 1 lemon
1 ciabatta loaf
4 pieces honeycomb
¼ cup orange blossom honey

Hop Butcher for the World

CHICAGO, ILLINOIS

The Pairing: Italian Pilsner

Savory and sweet with a full richness, this spread offers an unexpected way to wrap up a beer dinner and pairs wonderfully with an earthy, slightly spicy, hopped Italian pilsner. Created by Todd Davies and Laurie McNamara of Cadence Kitchen, these will go fast once they hit the table so make sure to save some for yourself.

In a blender or food processor, blend the ricotta, heavy cream, 1 tsp of the salt, and 1 tsp of the white pepper until well combined and smooth.

In a small pot, combine the olive oil, the garlic, the remaining 1 tsp of salt, and the remaining 1 tsp of white pepper. Place over low heat and steep for about 20 minutes, or until the garlic is light brown and soft. Remove from the heat. Transfer the garlic to a cutting board and crush it into a paste. Return the garlic to the pot and add 8 of the thyme sprigs and the lemon zest then stir to combine and allow to cool.

Preheat the oven to 500°F.

Cut the ciabatta into 1 in slices, put on baking sheet, and brush both sides liberally with about ½ cup of the roasted garlic oil. Toast in the oven for 2 minutes then flip and toast the other side for about 30 seconds, or until lightly browned.

Scoop the ricotta in the middle of a large plate and use a serving spoon to press it down in the middle. Place honeycomb pieces in the indentation, and top with the remaining 4 thyme sprigs. Drizzle with the honey and the remaining roasted garlic oil. Arrange the toasted ciabatta around the edges and serve immediately.

Hop Butcher for the World

The brewery began as a contract brand creating distinctive and flavorful IPAs that captured customer attention with their deft use of hopping and artistic labels. They were darlings of the beer festivals, with crowds lining up early for samples of their generously hopped IPAs, and store shelves would empty just as soon as they were stocked. Now, the brewery is planning a Chicago taproom to serve thirsty patrons on their own turf, hopefully with always-full tanks.

Hoppy Ales

ndia pale ale (IPA) is by far the most popular craft beer style today. It has evolved over the last forty or so years from an ale that was mostly malty, with a hop bite at the end, to brews that were all hop bitterness. Today, though, the style is a playground for brewers.

IPA is a term that is used to describe an overall hoppy beer, but it's important to understand this style's nuance and evolution. Hop-forward ales of moderate strength helped fuel the growth of this category. Dedicated drinkers were originally drawn to the assertive and punchy aromas and flavors brought out by lupulin, a sticky powder found inside hop cones. For a long time, bitter was the quality most commonly associated with IPAs, and that turned off many drinkers. But over the last few years, an evolution in the style has brought new fans into the fold and served as an introduction to craft beer for coming-of-age drinkers.

The IPA originated in England, where it was a well-hopped beer with a noticeable malt base. When the first generation of American craft brewers started making the style forty years ago, they turned up the dosage on the hops, trying to push the needle on the International Bitterness Unit (IBU) scale to new heights.

The West Coast IPA, also known as the American IPA, is often clear, and dark golden or copper in color, with classic hop aromas and flavors that can be described as pine- or grapefruit-forward and sometimes dank—hops are part of the cannabis family after all. Brewers typically add hops during the boil, extracting oils and imparting that desired bitterness, and use a more traditional grain bill (the grain makeup) of crystal malt and two-row malt, which is made from two-row barley.

Newer to the market, the New England–style IPA is celebrated for both its hazy look and juicy nature. Copious amounts of hops (pounds per barrel) are added to the beer, either after the wort has cooled or during the fermentation process, resulting in an intense, floral hop character with very little bitterness. This style uses traditional malts in its grain bill, but also benefits from the addition of oats and wheat for a fuller and softer mouthfeel.

Growers are regularly creating new hop varieties that impart a whole host of desirable aromas, but two of the most popular hops today, and ones you are mostly likely to see in descriptions, are Citra and Mosaic. Both are prized for their citrus and tropical fruit aromas and flavors.

Aside from hops, brewers are constantly experimenting with IPAs, adding fruit purées and lactose, playing with different yeast, including the fast-fermenting Norwegian strain Kviek, and even intentionally souring their beers. And innovation will only continue, so any drinker previously turned off by IPAs because of bitterness should give the new crop a fresh taste.

Despite being heavy on hops, IPAs are versatile when it comes to pairing with food. While they're assertive and can stand up to robust flavors like blue cheese, IPAs are also able to keep spicy heat at bay in Sichuan or Mexican dishes, and because of their inherent malt sweetness, they even pair well with desserts. IPAs made with modern hop varieties, especially ones that lean into tropical fruit flavors, are fun with sweets and vegetables, as well as some Asian dishes, and more earthy baked goods, like carrot cake.

Brewers use different hops in different ways and in different amounts, which makes experimentation key to drinking this style. Finding flavors that speak to your palate will help you find pairings that truly sing.

SPICY FISH CEVICHE WITH GRILLED PINEAPPLE

Serves 4 to 6

½ ripe golden pineapple, peeled and cut into ½ in rounds, with core intact
2 Tbsp vegetable oil
Kosher salt
1 lb fluke, halibut, or black bass, cut into ½ in dice
1½ cups fresh lime juice
¼ cup extra-virgin olive oil
1 small red onion, cut into ½ in dice
1 English cucumber, seeded and cut into ½ in dice
1 red bell pepper, seeded and cut into ½ in dice
1 jalepeño, seeded and minced
2 Tbsp ají amarillo paste
½ tsp ground cumin
⅓ cup chopped fresh cilantro

Springdale Beer Company

FRAMINGHAM, MASSACHUSETTS

The Pairing: Juicy West Coast IPA

This classic fish ceviche pairs wonderfully with the big tropical fruit aromas of a well-balanced, aromatic, and juicy IPA with West Coast–style bitterness. Chef Dave Punch, a Massachusetts restaurateur, says this ceviche will impress friends at any barbecue or party. He likes to serve his with grilled pineapple, because the fire changes the flavor of pineapple, giving it a "darker," less sweet flavor. A pineapple aroma certainly adds to the IPA experience. The ingredients call for ají amarillo paste, which is a yellow hot pepper paste typically from Peru. It can be found online, in Peruvian markets, and at some Mexican markets.

Preheat a grill to high.

Rub the pineapple rounds with the vegetable oil, season with 1 tsp salt, and grill, flipping occasionally, for about 6 minutes, or until dark grill marks appear on both sides. Transfer the pineapple to a cutting board and let cool then cut the rounds into ½ in pieces, removing the core as you chop.

In a nonreactive stainless steel or glass bowl, combine the fish and lime juice. Cover and refrigerate, stirring every 30 minutes or so, for 4 to 5 hours, or until the fish is opaque and doesn't look raw in the center. Strain off the lime juice and reserve. Rinse the fish under cold running water for 1 minute then return it to the bowl. Add the pineapple, olive oil, red onion, cucumber, bell pepper, jalapeño, ají amarillo paste, and cumin and gently toss to combine. Add the cilantro and 2 tsp of salt and the reserved lime juice and gently toss to combine. Serve in small bowls or wide-mouthed stemmed glassware.

Springdale Beer Company

After years of exclusively making lagers, the brothers behind Jack's Abby decided to get into the ale game. Springdale beers are made in the same building as their lager-focused operation. This is where the brewers and Hendler brothers experiment with IPAs and an extensive barrel-aging program, where cocktail-inspired beers, strong whisky-infused stouts, and more are created. A dedicated spot to enjoy Springdale beers is located in nearby Brighton, Massachusetts.

MUSHROOM AND VEGETABLE DUMPLINGS WITH MANGO CHILI NUOC CHAM

Serves 4 to 6

DUMPLINGS

3 Tbsp sesame oil

1 lb mushrooms, such as shiitake, cremini, oyster, or button, trimmed and thinly sliced

1 lb carrots, peeled and cut into small dice

1 lb napa cabbage, thinly sliced

3 scallions, thinly sliced, plus more for serving (optional)

2 garlic cloves, minced

2 Tbsp freshly grated ginger

3 Tbsp tamari

2 Tbsp black vinegar or rice vinegar

1 Tbsp dried chile flakes, preferably gochugaru (Korean red chile flakes)

2 tsp granulated sugar

2 tsp kosher salt

1 tsp freshly ground black pepper

continues ↗

Drekker Brewing Co.

FARGO, NORTH DAKOTA

The Pairing: New England–style IPA

The citrus and often tropical notes found in hazy New England–style IPAs play perfectly with the ginger and mango in these easy to make and wonderfully presented Korean-style dumplings. This recipe by chefs Ryan Nitschke and Luna Fargo relies on a fusion of Asian flavors. They're served with nuoc cham, a simple Vietnamese dipping sauce that delivers both sweetness and spice.

To make the dumplings: In a large sauté pan or skillet, heat the sesame oil over medium-high heat. Add the mushrooms, carrots, and cabbage and cook, stirring occasionally, for 3 to 5 minutes, or until softened. Add the scallions, garlic, and ginger and cook for 2 more minutes, or until the vegetables are cooked but still slightly crunchy and the mixture is aromatic. Transfer to a large bowl and let cool slightly. Add the tamari, vinegar, chili flakes, sugar, salt, and pepper and set aside.

When ready to assemble the dumplings, fill a small bowl with water. Keeping the wrappers under a damp towel while you work, dip one finger into the water and dampen the outer edges of a pot sticker wrapper. Place a heaping tablespoon of the filling in the middle. Carefully fold the dumpling to create a half-moon shape and gently but firmly press the edges together to tightly seal. Starting at one corner, use your thumb and pointer finger to fold over and pleat the edge of the dumpling, gently pressing the pleat to seal. Repeat to create several more pleats around the edge of the dumpling. Repeat this process with the remaining pot sticker wrappers and filling.

In a large cast-iron or nonstick pan, heat 2 Tbsp of the canola oil over medium-high heat. Add 5 to 6 dumplings to the pan and fry for 2 minutes then flip the dumplings and fry for 2 more minutes, or until beginning to brown. Add just enough water to cover the bottom of the pan then

> *Drekker Brewing Co*
> *This Viking-themed brewery from the great north has been leading the charge on hop innovation in American IPAs for the last several years. From running trials on hopping rates to coaxing out often elusive flavors, Drekker has gained fans in the upper Midwest and beyond with their branding, bold flavors, and creativity.*

24 gyoza won ton skins or
    pot sticker wrappers
Canola or other neutral oil
Kimchi (optional)
Fresh cilantro (optional)

NUOC CHAM
½ cup rice vinegar
¼ cup fish sauce
¼ cup granulated sugar
1 mango, peeled and
    finely diced
1 Tbsp sambal oelek
1 tsp minced garlic
Juice of 1 lime
1 tsp kosher salt
1 Tbsp arrowroot or
    cornstarch

cover, turn the heat to medium-low, and steam the dumplings for about 5 minutes, or until the water has evaporated. Remove the cover and allow the dumplings to sit in pan for about 3 to 5 minutes, or until golden brown and slightly crisp. Repeat to cook the remaining dumplings, adding more oil and water for each batch.

To make the nuoc cham: In a small saucepan, combine the vinegar, fish sauce, sugar, and 1 cup of water and bring to a simmer over medium heat. Continue simmering, stirring, until the sugar is dissolved. Add the mango, sambal oelek, garlic, lime juice, and salt and return to a simmer.

In a small bowl, combine the arrowroot and 2 Tbsp water and whisk to dissolve. Add to the mango mixture and simmer, whisking, for about 1 minute, or until thickened. Remove from the heat and enjoy warm or at room temperature.

Eat dumplings immediately dipped in the nuoc cham. For a more complete presentation, arrange the dumplings on a serving plate and top with kimchi (if using). Spoon the nuoc cham over the dumplings and finish with a sprinkle of sliced scallions and cilantro (if using).

SPICY BRUSSELS SPROUTS

Serves 2 to 4

¾ cup smooth peanut butter
½ cup Thai sweet chili sauce, such as Mae Ploy
1 Tbsp Sriracha
Peanut oil, for frying
1 lb Brussels sprouts, trimmed and cut lengthwise in half
Kosher salt
¼ cup chopped peanuts

Weathered Souls Brewing Co.

SAN ANTONIO, TEXAS

The Pairing: West Coast IPA

Here is further proof that Brussels sprouts need not be boring or bland. When served with a spicy and sweet sauce, lightly fried, and given extra texture with a peanut garnish, these can be a meal on their own. When paired with a West Coast IPA, the beer helps tamp down some of the spiciness but also brings out the earthy flavor of the sprouts. A word of advice: have a splatter guard or lid ready as soon as the sprouts hit the oil—they are going to pop and sizzle.

In a blender, combine the peanut butter, chili sauce, and Sriracha and blend on high until smooth. Set aside.

Line a plate with paper towels. In a large skillet, heat ½ in of peanut oil over medium-high until sizzling. Add the Brussels sprouts and fry, using a splatter guard, stirring occasionally, for 2 minutes, or until the outsides develop a brown crust but aren't burnt. Transfer to the paper towel–lined plate to drain then transfer to a serving bowl and season with salt. Add the sauce and toss to evenly coat the sprouts. Sprinkle with the peanuts and serve immediately.

> **Weathered Souls Brewing Co.**
> *Though based in Texas, Weathered Souls has a global impact. In the wake of the murder of George Floyd in 2020, head brewer Marcus Baskerville spearheaded the Black Is Beautiful beer initiative, which created an open-source imperial stout recipe that was brewed across the country and around the world, with proceeds supporting local social justice causes.*

MERGUEZ SPICED LAMB BURGER

Serves 4

2 lbs ground lamb
¼ cup red wine
1½ Tbsp chopped garlic
1½ tsp Hungarian paprika
1½ tsp kosher salt
1½ tsp freshly ground
    black pepper
½ tsp dried oregano
½ tsp red pepper flakes
8 roasted red pepper strips,
    jarred or fresh
4 slices fresh mozzarella, cut
    into ½ in rounds
4 brioche buns or Kaiser rolls,
    well toasted
Chipotle mayo, for serving

Reuben's Brews

SEATTLE, WASHINGTON

The Pairing: Imperial or Triple IPA

This burger is spicy, juicy, and calls for a strong, hoppy pale ale. An assertive imperial IPA that's big on abv, as well as citrus and pine hop flavor, should keep all that heat in check. At Brouwer's Café in Seattle, where this recipe originates, they use boneless lamb shoulder and grind it in house to get the perfect mix, but it's just fine to use preground lamb. If you do have a meat grinder at home, marinate the meat in the wine overnight. The next day, grind the meat, garlic, and wine once using a ⅜ in plate, then thoroughly mix in the spices by hand and grind the mixture once more.

In a large bowl, combine the ground lamb, wine, garlic, paprika, salt, pepper, oregano, and red pepper flakes. Mix thoroughly and form into four 8 oz patties. Transfer to a plate, cover with plastic wrap, and refrigerate for at least 1 hour and up to 12 hours.

When ready to serve, heat a charcoal or gas grill to 450°F. Grill the burgers to your preferred doneness—about 5 minutes for medium—then flip them, top with the roasted red peppers and mozzarella, and continue cooking for 3 to 4 more minutes. Place the burgers on the toasted bottom buns then smear the tops of the buns with chipotle mayo, close the burgers, and serve immediately.

Reuben's Brews

After continually racking up awards as a home brewer, Adam Robbings decided to leave his corporate day job behind and go pro with his passion for beer. He named the brewery after his son, and since 2012, it has grown into one of the most respected breweries in the Pacific Northwest. Originally from London, Adam brings an English sensibility to his recipes, which are well balanced and often traditional but sometimes experimental. The brewery's taproom is an open and welcoming space, a spot to grab a few pints with friends and watch football (the proper kind).

BRINED PORK CHOPS WITH MAPLE GLAZE AND APPLE CHUTNEY

Serves 4

PORK

4 bone-in pork chops,
    10 to 12 oz each
2 cups lager or IPA
⅓ cup kosher salt
3 garlic cloves, crushed
2 bay leaves
½ tsp red pepper flakes
Freshly ground black pepper

GLAZE

1 cup maple syrup
2 chipotle chiles in adobo
½ tsp kosher salt
3 Tbsp unsalted butter,
    melted

continues ↗

SingleSpeed Brewing Company

WATERLOO, IOWA

The Pairing: American IPA

Straight from America's heartland, this pork dish benefits from a day-long brine, which tenderizes the meat while adding flavor. Plan this for a weekend meal when time is on your side, and family dinner around the table is achievable. The chops pair well with the Honey Glazed Carrots (following recipe).

To brine the pork chops: Put the pork chops in a 9 by 13 in baking dish so they lay flat and don't overlap. In a large bowl, whisk together 2 cups of water, the beer, salt, garlic, bay leaves, and red pepper flakes until the salt is dissolved. Pour over the pork chops, cover with plastic wrap, and brine in the refrigerator for 12 to 24 hours.

To make the glaze: In a blender or food processor, combine the maple syrup, chipotle chiles, and salt and blend until combined. With the blender or processor running, slowly stream in the melted butter, blending until the sauce is emulsified and thickens slightly.

SingleSpeed Brewing Company
A lot of breweries talk about sustainable practices, but SingleSpeed in eastern Iowa puts it into practice. With both large- and small-scale initiatives aimed at reducing waste, using natural resources, like wind and solar power, to produce beer, each pint you drink from their two breweries is helping to make the planet a better place.

¼ cup white vinegar

¼ cup light brown sugar

½ lb Granny Smith apples, peeled, cored, and cut into small dice

½ Tbsp lemon juice

1 garlic clove, minced

½ tsp mustard seeds

½ tsp freshly grated ginger

¼ tsp red pepper flakes

⅛ tsp coriander seeds

Pinch of ground allspice

Pinch of cayenne pepper

Kosher salt

To make the chutney: In a medium saucepan, bring the vinegar and brown sugar to a simmer over medium heat. Continue simmering, stirring occasionally, for 5 minutes, or until the brown sugar is dissolved. Add the apples, lemon juice, garlic, mustard seeds, ginger, red pepper flakes, coriander, allspice, cayenne, and salt and return to a simmer. Continue simmering for 3 minutes, or until apples begin to soften then turn the heat to low and cook, stirring occasionally, for 20 to 30 minutes, or until the apples are slightly darker. Keep warm until ready to serve.

When ready to serve, heat a gas or charcoal grill to 450°F.

Remove the pork chops from the brine, pat dry with a paper towel, and lightly season with salt and pepper. Grill the pork chops, flipping 3 times, for 2 to 3 minutes per side, or until the internal temperature of the chops reaches 145°F. Remove from the grill, brush with the glaze, and allow to rest for 5 to 10 minutes. Serve the pork chops with the chutney on top or on the side.

HONEY GLAZED CARROTS

Serves 4 to 6

1 lb carrots, peeled and cut into 1 in pieces

¼ cup honey

½ tsp dried sage

Fine sea salt

2 Tbsp unsalted butter, cold

Preheat the oven to 400°F.

Put the carrots in a small baking dish and add just enough water so they are half submerged. Cover with aluminum foil and bake for about 45 minutes, or until the carrots are tender when pierced with a fork.

Meanwhile, in a small saucepan, bring the honey to a gentle boil over medium-high heat then immediately remove from the heat. Add the sage and season with salt. Slowly add the cold butter, stirring until emulsified into a sauce. Keep warm.

Once the carrots are tender, drain any excess water. Add the honey glaze, toss to coat, and serve with the Brined Pork Chops (previous recipe).

SPAETZLE AND BEERCHAMEL CHEESE SAUCE

Serves 4

SAUCE

3 Tbsp unsalted butter
3 Tbsp all-purpose flour
½ cup whole milk
½ cup heavy cream
¾ cup beer, preferably lager
    or cream ale
2 cups shredded cheese
½ tsp chili powder
½ tsp paprika
Fine sea salt and freshly
    ground black pepper

SPAETZLE

1½ cups all-purpose flour
1 cup whole milk
3 large eggs
1 tsp fine sea salt

SingleSpeed Brewing Company

WATERLOO, IOWA

The Pairing: Oktoberfest

Serve this beer-infused cheesy spaetzle with the Brined Pork Chop with Maple Glaze and Apple Chutney (page 48), or skip the cheese sauce and enjoy the spaetzle alongside the Jägerschnitzel (page 30). SingleSpeed uses a mixture of American smoked Gouda, Cheddar cheese, and cheese curds to make the sauce, but you can use any cheese or combination of cheeses.

To make the sauce: In a medium saucepan, melt the butter over medium heat. Stir in the flour to create a roux. Continue cooking and stirring for about 6 minutes, or until the roux is slightly darkened and has a nutty aroma. Slowly add the milk, heavy cream, and beer, stirring constantly for about 2 to 4 minutes, or until the sauce starts to thicken. Add the cheese and stir until melted and fully incorporated. Add the chili powder and paprika and season with salt and pepper.

To make the spaetzle: In a large bowl, whisk together the flour, milk, eggs, and salt until a thick batter forms.

In a large pot, bring about 6 quarts of water to a rolling boil.

Using a spaetzle maker, pour about half the batter into the top compartment and slide the cup back and forth to allow the batter to drop through and into the boiling water. Pour the remaining batter into the cup and repeat the process, moving quickly until all the batter is cooking in the pot. Give the spaetzle dumplings a good stir then let them cook for 1 to 2 minutes, or until they float to the surface. Using a slotted spoon, transfer the spaetzle dumplings to a serving bowl, add the cheese sauce, and toss to coat. Serve warm.

GAENG HANG LAE

Serves 4

CURRY PASTE

6 to 10 small dried chiles

6 garlic cloves

4 Thai shallots or pearl
  onions, peeled and roughly
  chopped

1 lemongrass stalk, trimmed
  and roughly chopped

1 in piece galangal, cut into
  ¼ in thick rounds

1 tsp kapi (fermented
  shrimp paste)

1 tsp fine sea salt

2 tsp freshly grated or dried
  turmeric

1 tsp whole black peppercorns

2 tsp garam masala or curry
  powder

PORK BELLY

2 lbs pork belly, cut into
  large chunks

1 cup pearl onions, peeled

10 garlic cloves, peeled

¼ cup palm sugar

2 Tbsp dark soy sauce
  or kecap manis

2 Tbsp fish sauce

2 Tbsp tamarind concentrate

Cooked jasmine rice,
  for serving

½ in piece fresh ginger, peeled
  and cut into matchsticks

Fresh dill, for serving
  (optional)

Hopewell Brewing Co.

CHICAGO, ILLINOIS

The Pairing: Pale Ale

Sumptuous without being overpowering, this braised pork belly curry is a beloved northern Thai dish. Coconutless, it's also rich in dried spices and fresh herbs, revealing a Burmese influence. As with most stews, it tastes even better the next day. Chef Palita Sriratana, the owner of Pink Salt in Chicago, says the back notes are a balance of tamarind, fish sauce, and palm sugar. Pair it with a pale ale and the earthy undertones of the beer will boost the spice in the stew.

To make the curry paste: In a small bowl, cover the dried chiles with warm water and soak for 30 minutes. Drain the chiles and transfer to a stone mortar. Add the garlic, shallots, lemongrass, galangal, kapi, and salt and grind with pestle until combined. Add the turmeric, peppercorns, and garam masala and pound until a smooth paste forms. (Alternatively, combine the ingredients in a blender with ¼ cup of water.)

To make the pork belly: In a large Dutch oven or other heavy pot, cook the pork belly over medium heat, turning as needed, for 10 minutes, or until browned on all sides. Add the curry paste and fry, stirring frequently to avoid burning the pork, for about 1 minute, or until fragrant. Cover with 6 cups of water and bring to a low simmer. Add the pearl onions and garlic and continue simmering for 40 minutes, or until the pork belly is tender, some of the fat has rendered out, and the sauce has thickened—the dish should have the consistency of a stew or gravy. Add the palm sugar, dark soy sauce, fish sauce, and tamarind and stir to incorporate.

Serve with jasmine rice and sprinkle with ginger and dill (if using).

Hopewell Brewing Co.

The founders of the brewery see it as a progressive endeavor. It's not just a place where beer is made but where friendships are forged and plans are made to better society. From social justice initiatives to discussions and actions to promote diversity, Hopewell is a gathering spot for good that also makes really good beer.

THE ADULT PEANUT BUTTER AND JELLY SANDWICH

Makes 1 sandwich

2 Tbsp freshly ground or high-quality jarred nut butter

2 slices Texas toast or similar thickly sliced white bread

2 Tbsp fruit preserves

1 tsp chili garlic paste

1 16 oz bag lard-fried potato chips

Bonn Place Brewing Co.

BETHLEHEM, PENNSYLVANIA

The Pairing: Extra Special Bitter

The classic peanut butter and jelly sandwich is a lot like a beer journey. As kids, we begin with the basics—white bread, familiar brands, no crust. Then our palates evolve, and we get more creative with our PB&J choices. Beer is the same way. We start off with American light lager then discover there is more to beer and try new styles.

This recipe from Sam Masotto, owner and head brewer of Bonn Place Brewing Co., relies on artisanal nut butter and fruit preserves, making it a step up from the ubiquitous spreads, and perfect for adults who want to feel like kids again. At the brewery, they offer this sandwich "Jazzy Style," with potato chips and a thin layer of chili garlic paste, but you should follow your palate to create your own flavor combinations—just be sure to seek out high-quality ingredients. ESB (extra special bitter), or a similar English-style mild, makes an excellent pairing, preferably one with a sweet, nutty characteristic and slightly earthy hops.

Spread the nut butter generously on 1 slice of bread. Spread the fruit preserves on the other slice and then top with the chili garlic paste. Arrange about a quarter of the potato chips on top of the nut butter. Close the sandwich and serve with more chips.

> **Bonn Place Brewing Co.**
> *Creativity abounds at this eastern Pennsylvania brewery. Helmed by stage actor Sam Masotto, it has been producing quality, quaffable pints for several years inside a small space with an English pub feel. From their award-winning milds and ESB to creative twists on classics, Bonn Place has become a destination for beer fans looking for whimsy and tradition. They've also created a universe of characters through their Instagram account, which is thoroughly entertaining to follow.*

CITRUS TRES LECHES CAKE WITH ORANGE BLOSSOM AND BASIL

Serves 6 to 8

ORANGE BLOSSOM SYRUP
¾ cup granulated sugar
1 cup heavy cream
¼ cup orange blossom water
1 tsp pure vanilla extract

CITRUS CAKE
1 cup all-purpose flour
½ tsp baking soda
½ tsp baking powder
½ tsp fine sea salt
½ cup packed coconut oil,
    at room temperature
1 cup granulated sugar
1 tsp pure vanilla extract
4 large eggs, separated
¼ cup plus 2 Tbsp buttermilk
Zest of 2 lemons
1 Tbsp fresh lemon juice

LEMON CURD
⅓ cup granulated sugar
⅓ cup fresh lemon juice
2 large eggs
1 Tbsp unsalted butter, at
    room temperature

continues ↗

Edmund's Oast Brewing Co.

CHARLESTON, SOUTH CAROLINA

The Pairing: American IPA

Tres leches is a sponge cake typically soaked with a combination of three milks, hence the name. This version, created by Heather Hutton, the pastry chef for the Restaurant at Edmund's Oast, is soaked instead with orange blossom water and cream and then finished with fresh grapefruit, lemon, and basil. Pair it with a citrus-forward American IPA.

To make the orange blossom syrup: In a small saucepan, bring the granulated sugar and 1 cup of water to a boil over high heat. Remove from the heat and allow to cool. Add the heavy cream, orange blossom water, and vanilla and whisk to incorporate. Cover and chill until ready to serve.

To make the citrus cake: Preheat the oven to 350°F. Coat an 8 in round aluminum cake pan with cooking spray, line the bottom with parchment paper, and spray the paper. Dust the inside of the pan with flour, making sure to cover the entire pan.

In a medium bowl, whisk together the flour, baking soda, baking powder, and salt. Set aside.

In the bowl of a stand mixer fitted with a paddle attachment, or using a handheld mixer, beat the coconut oil and ½ cup of the granulated sugar on medium for about 5 minutes, or until fluffy.

In a small bowl, add the vanilla to the egg yolks without stirring. Add the yolks, one at a time, to the coconut oil mixture and beat on medium, scraping down the sides of the bowl as needed, until fully incorporated.

In another small bowl, combine the buttermilk, zest, and lemon juice.

Add the flour mixture to the coconut oil mixture in four additions, alternating with the buttermilk-and-lemon mixture and ending with the flour. Mix until just combined and then transfer to a new large bowl.

Thoroughly wash and dry the bowl of the stand mixer or the mixing bowl if using a handheld mixer. Add the egg whites and start whipping with the whisk attachment or handheld mixer until soft peaks form— the egg whites will turn white and start to show lines. Gradually add the remaining ½ cup granulated sugar, 1 tablespoon at a time,

ORANGE BLOSSOM ICING

¾ cup heavy cream

2 Tbsp confectioners' sugar

1½ Tbsp orange blossom
  water

1 tsp pure vanilla extract

ASSEMBLY

1 grapefruit

2 oranges, preferably navel
  or blood orange

2 lemons

Basil sprigs

Edmund's Oast

It's hard not to have a good time at this expansive Charleston brewery and taproom. With a kitchen that excels with fresh and inventive takes on classic dishes, a hospitality staff that is top notch, and beers that push boundaries, Edmund's Oast is a place you'll visit once and then again as often as possible.

and whip until shiny, stiff peaks form. Add about a third of the whipped egg whites to the cake batter and gently fold to incorporate. Add the remaining whipped egg whites and gently fold until no streaks remain. Pour into the prepared pan and bake for about 1 hour, or until the center of the cake bounces back when touched. Run a thin knife or metal spatula around the edges of the pan to prevent sticking then let the cake cool in the pan for 1 hour.

To make the lemon curd: In a small saucepan, combine the granulated sugar, lemon juice, and eggs over medium heat. Cook, whisking constantly, for about 3 minutes, or until the eggs start to thicken. Pour through a fine mesh strainer set over a bowl; discard any solids. Add the butter, whisk to incorporate, cover, and refrigerate until cold.

To soak the cake: When the cake is completely cool (do not remove it from the pan), use a skewer to poke a dozen holes across the top. Slowly pour the orange blossom syrup over the cake, allowing it to be completely absorbed. Tightly cover the cake pan with plastic wrap and refrigerate for 5 to 8 hours.

To make the orange blossom icing: In the bowl of a stand mixer fitted with the whisk attachment or using a handheld mixer, whip the heavy cream and confectioners' sugar together until soft yet sturdy peaks form. Fold in the orange blossom water and vanilla, cover, and refrigerate until ready to use.

To assemble the cake: Run an icing spatula around the edges of the cake pan then carefully flip the cake onto a serving plate or platter—you may have to tap the sides of the pan, but the cake will slowly come out. Peel off the parchment paper. Using an icing spatula, spread the frosting across the top of the cake. Add the lemon curd to the center of cake and spread it to thinly to cover the top but leave a small border of icing around the edges.

Remove the skin from the grapefruit, oranges, and lemons. Cut the grapefruit and oranges crosswise into slices then cut each slice into halves or quarters. Cut the lemons into segments. Arrange the fruit on top of the cake then place basil sprigs in between the pieces of citrus. The cake can be refrigerated for up to 3 days.

Belgian-Style Ales

A glass of Belgian-style ale is a meal in itself. Developed over centuries of tinkering, improving, and innovating, Belgian-style ales rely heavily on malts, spices, and yeast to impart deep and nuanced flavor that's made for enjoying with food and can be adapted for any meal or occasion.

From their easy-drinking lagers and light and fruity blonde ales to their various stronger ales, the Belgians have learned to match flavor intensities and find commonalities between what's in the glass and what's on the plate. A whole universe of styles was born within this small country's borders and from the coast to the cities to the farms, Belgian beers often play off local flavors. In fact, the saying "if it grows together, it goes together" serves as a particularly helpful way to find a satisfying pairing for Belgian beer.

A Belgian-style dubbel has chocolate and roasted aromas derived from malt, while a tripel, lighter in color but higher in abv, features aromas of spices. With a fuller body, it pairs well with seafood. A quad is a monster of a beer, both in terms of alcohol and flavor, imparting stone fruit and brown sugar notes. Quads are an ideal partner for fatty meats like duck, as well as cooked fruits and rich desserts.

Then there are saisons, which are sometimes known as farmhouse ales. While brewed with wheat, they are Belgian in origin and synonymous with the country. (For more wheat-forward beers and pairings, see page 99.) Saisons are lightly spicy, medium-bodied, complex, and ideal for enjoying with food. On Thanksgiving, they're a utility player, perfect for pairing with herb roasted turkey, roasted sweet potatoes, and oyster stuffing, and able to highlight the attributes of each. For regular nights at home, saisons, especially ones with an aged, earthy hop character, pair beautifully with sweet and tangy barbecue, as well as roasted vegetables.

Belgium is also home to lambic and gueuze, spontaneously fermented ales using ambient yeast and other microbes. (For additional recipes that pair with those styles, see Wild Beers on page 159.)

American brewers have taken these styles and adapted them for modern palates. This can mean variations brewed with chocolate or aged in spirit barrels, but it can also mean aggressively hopped beers that challenge the balance and delicate nature of these beers. When searching the shelves for Belgian-style beers to pair with your next meal, look to local or regional breweries that have a healthy respect for tradition, ingredients, and methods. Or, simply stroll down the import aisle to get the real McCoy.

FRESH OYSTERS WITH MIGNONETTE AND COCKTAIL SAUCE

Makes 1 cup of mignonette and 2 cups cocktail sauce

MIGNONETTE

2 medium shallots, minced
1½ Tbsp whole black
    peppercorns, toasted and
    freshly ground
1 cup red wine vinegar
1 Tbsp balsamic vinegar

COCKTAIL SAUCE

1½ cups ketchup
½ cup freshly grated
    horseradish
2 Tbsp Worcestershire sauce
Juice of ½ lemon
1 Tbsp hot sauce, such
    as Tabasco or similar
    hot sauce
2 dozen oysters, freshly
    shucked and on ice

Eventide Oyster Co. Allagash Brewing Company

PORTLAND, MAINE

The Pairing: Tripel

At Eventide, a beloved oyster bar in Portland, Maine, there is a dedicated tap handle for Allagash Tripel, a beer Eventide's owner Arlin Smith calls the perfect pairing with oysters. Allagash, another Portland establishment, helped introduce Belgian-style beers to thirsty American drinkers when they opened in 1995.

"We serve oysters in a simple way, with cocktail sauce and mignonette, and because of its alcohol content, a tripel adds some body to a light taste," says Smith. "That extra body really pushes the boundaries of a briny, mineral oyster." He goes further, explaining that the subtle fruitiness in a tripel brings out the same in oysters. The tripel also stands up to the heat from horseradish and helps calm some of the acidity in the mignonette.

To pick good oysters, Smith recommends trusting your source and your nose. In the same way that we've evolved to avoid sushi from a gas station, know your purveyor. Find a local seafood market close to home or get overnight shipping from places like Eventide. Oysters shouldn't smell fishy but should be bright and salty, like the ocean. Discard any that don't pass the sniff test, because even the strongest of Belgian ales can't save you from bad shellfish.

These two garnishes can be used in small dabs atop freshly shucked oysters.

To make the mignonette: In a small bowl, whisk together the shallots, freshly ground toasted peppercorns, red wine vinegar, and balsamic vinegar. Cover and refrigerate for at least 1 hour or overnight to let the flavors mingle. The mignonette can be refrigerated in an airtight container for up to 1 month.

To make the cocktail sauce: In a small bowl, whisk together the ketchup, horseradish, Worcestershire sauce, lemon juice, and hot sauce. Serve immediately or refrigerate until ready to use. The cocktail sauce can be refrigerated in an airtight container for up to 1 month.

Plate fresh oysters over crushed ice and top with sauce or mignonette as desired.

Allagash Brewing Company

One of the country's largest craft brewers, Allagash became a fan favorite on the back of its white ale, a Belgian-inspired witbier. The brewery's motto, "Innovation: Continually pushing the limits of beer and ourselves," is painted on a brewery wall and is clearly evident in each of its beers. Eventide Oyster Co. honors seafood traditions and the natural flavors of the sea, while sometimes adding modern twists. Together, these two companies are at the top of the list of reasons to visit Portland, Maine.

"STEAK AND EGGS"

Serves 4

CURED EGG YOLKS
1 lb kosher salt
4 large eggs

BEEF TARTARE
1 lb beef tenderloin
1 small shallot, minced
¼ cup minced fresh
    flat-leaf parsley
4 tsp capers
3 Tbsp olive oil
Kosher salt and freshly
    ground black pepper
½ habanero, seeded and
    minced
1 cup yellow mustard
½ cup honey
1 baguette
4 tsp caviar
Microgreens, for serving
2 oz banana ketchup,
    for serving

Wolf's Ridge Brewing
COLUMBUS, OHIO

The Pairing: Dubbel

This clever take on steak and eggs, created by Seth Lassak, executive chef for Wolf's Ridge, is labor intensive and requires starting two days in advance. But it is well worth the extra time and effort. Featuring beef tartare and cured egg yolks, it combines traditional flavors with creative new twists like habanero honey mustard and banana ketchup that really pop on the palate. Pair it with a dubbel. With its light roasted chocolate notes, this Belgian beer will tone down the heat and complement the meat, while adding a subtle fruity touch to every bite. Buy the freshest, highest quality beef tenderloin you can find and look for banana ketchup in your grocery store's international section.

To make the cured eggs: About 43 hours before you plan to serve this dish, fill a shallow pan with most of the kosher salt. Carefully crack the eggs to separate the yolks from the whites and so that you can use the eggshells as nests for the yolks. Reserve the whites for another use. Place the yolks in the eggshells then gently put the filled eggshells in the bed of salt. Carefully top the yolks with the remaining salt until completely buried. Cover and refrigerate for 40 hours.

Preheat the oven to 150°F. Line a baking sheet with parchment paper.

Remove the cured yolks, which should be firm, from the salt and gently rinse under cold running water. Transfer the yolks to the prepared baking sheet and bake, turning and rotating every 20 minutes, for 3 hours, or until dried. Remove from the oven and allow to cool.

Wolf's Ridge Brewing
This Columbus, Ohio, brewery and restaurant has a deep appreciation for tradition and innovation, looking to time-honored methods of beer making but also using unique flavors to breathe new life and dimension into each pint they create. From a robust barrel aging program to fruit-infused sours, Wolf's Ridge makes beers that get the analytical parts of the brain working overtime.

To make the beef tartare: Preheat the oven to 350°F.

If you have a grinder, grind the beef tenderloin. Alternatively, finely chop it with a sharp knife. Put the ground beef in a small bowl and add the shallot, parsley, capers, and 1 Tbsp of the olive oil. Season with salt and pepper and gently toss to combine.

In a second small bowl, combine the habanero, mustard, and honey.

Cut the baguette into thin slices and put on a baking sheet. Drizzle with the remaining 2 Tbsp of olive oil and season with salt and pepper. Bake for 5 to 7 minutes, or until slightly browned and crispy. Allow to cool.

Gently pack the beef tartare mixture into a 2 or 3 in mold to create a round patty in the center of a serving platter or plate. Using a microplane, shave some of the cured egg yolk on top of the beef tartare then place the caviar on top. Sprinkle with the microgreens. Drizzle the habanero honey mustard on the plate and dot the banana ketchup around the edges. Enjoy with the crostini.

A BETTER CAESAR SALAD

Serves 4

DRESSING

½ cup olive oil
8 boquerones (marinated white anchovies)
6 black garlic cloves
¼ cup freshly grated Parmigiano-Reggiano, plus additional for serving
1 tsp Dijon mustard
1 tsp capers
1 tsp Worcestershire sauce
1 large egg yolk
Freshly ground black pepper

CHEESE PUFFS

¼ lb piece Parmigiano-Reggiano rind, cut into ½ in pieces

SALAD

4 cups baby arugula
Maldon sea salt flakes and freshly ground black pepper

Primitive Beer

LONGMONT, COLORADO

The Pairing: Lambic

The tart and lively characteristics of lambic, a hopped-up spontaneously fermented ale, inspired this creative approach to a classic dish. Anthony W. Lopiccolo, chef and owner of Goed Zuur in Denver, says he wanted to craft an umami bomb with backbone to intersect the beer's acid structure. Texture is everything when it comes to salad, and this recipe provides the juxtaposing layers of crunchiness and creaminess required to make a bowl of greens stand out and not get lost in a beer pairing. The use of Parmigiano-Reggiano rinds, baked to puffs, as a garnish should also get some attention.

To make the dressing: Line a plate with paper towels. In a medium sauté pan, heat ¼ cup of the olive oil over medium heat. Add the boquerones and sauté for 5 minutes, or until lightly browned. Transfer the boquerones to the paper towel–lined plate to drain. Combine the olive oil with the remaining ¼ cup of fresh olive oil and allow to cool to room temperature.

In a small bowl, combine the black garlic, Parmigiano-Reggiano, mustard, capers, Worcestershire sauce, and egg yolk with an immersion blender. With the blender running, slowly add the cooled olive oil, blending until the dressing is emulsified. Add 1 Tbsp of water and blend to ensure the dressing stays emulsified. Season with pepper.

To make the cheese puffs: Preheat the oven to 350°F. Line a baking sheet with parchment paper.

Put the pieces of Parmigiano-Reggiano rind 1 in apart on the prepared baking sheet. Bake for 10 to 20 minutes, or until the pieces have puffed and are cooked through the center. Allow to cool.

To make the salad: Put the arugula in a large bowl. Gradually add the dressing and use your hands to mix and toss the greens until they are coated to your liking. Add the cheese puffs and mix again. Divide the salad among plates and top with two anchovies and additional grated Parmigiano-Reggiano. Season with Maldon sea salt and pepper.

Primitive Beer

Lisa and Brandon Boldt, the owners of Primitive Beer in Colorado, bill themselves as Colorado's first exclusively spontaneous, barrel-fermented beer blendery. And in a state that has claimed its fair share of firsts, that's a pretty big deal, especially once you taste their beer. When they opened their doors in 2018, the Boldts made a splash on the local scene with their Méthode Traditionnelle (an American term for lambic) ales, as well as their packaging—maybe you've seen their beer in a box. But their bottled offerings are also starting to pop up around the country and would certainly be coveted at bottle shares.

ROASTED MUSHROOM AND GARLIC BISQUE WITH PAN TOASTED BAGUETTE

Fogtown Brewing Company

ELLSWORTH & BAR HARBOR, MAINE

The Pairing: Saison

This pairing, which brings together mushrooms and saison, is all about the umami experience. The brewery recommends its "seaweed saison," which is brewed with Maine-grown organic wheat, oat and spelt from Maine Grain, locally harvested dulse, kelp, and Irish moss seaweeds, and then fermented with *Brettanomyces*. You should be able to find a local savory saison that pairs just as well, as many brewers are experimenting with alternative grains and umami ingredients in their beers.

Preheat the oven to 400°F. Line a baking sheet with parchment paper.

Add the mushrooms to the prepared baking sheet, drizzle with 2 Tbsp of the olive oil and toss to coat. Cut the head of garlic horizontally in half and rub both cut sides with 1 Tbsp of the olive oil. Add to the baking sheet with the mushrooms and roast for 20 minutes, or until the mushrooms start to brown at the edges. Continue to roast the garlic, as needed, until browned all over. Let the garlic cool and once it's cool enough to handle, peel it and discard the skins.

In a small bowl, whisk together the light cream and cornstarch until no lumps remain. Set aside.

In a deep pot, combine two-thirds of the mushrooms with the peeled roasted garlic, the vegetable stock, and black and white pepper, if using. Use an immersion blender or food processor to purée until smooth then place over medium heat and bring to a boil. Slowly incorporate the cream and cornstarch slurry, stirring continuously. Return to a boil and continue boiling until the soup is thick, about 1 minute. Stir in the rest of the mushrooms and the fresh thyme.

When ready to serve, heat a medium skillet over medium heat. Spread butter on one side of each baguette slice then add to the skillet, buttered-side down, and toast for 2 to 3 minutes, or until golden brown.

Divide the bisque among bowls and serve hot with the toasted baguette.

Serves 6

1 lb wild mushrooms, preferably oyster, trumpet, and lion's mane, cut into bite-size pieces
4 Tbsp mild extra-virgin olive oil
1 head garlic
¼ cup plus 2 Tbsp light cream
2 Tbsp cornstarch
4½ cups vegetable stock
¼ tsp freshly ground black pepper
⅛ tsp freshly ground white pepper (optional)
3 sprigs fresh thyme
1 baguette, halved horizontally and cut into 8 slices
4 Tbsp (½ stick) unsalted butter, at room temperature

Fogtown Brewing Company

Maine is both a vacation paradise and a beer destination, and when visitors flock to its mountains and rocky shores they are looking for fresh air, nature, and an escape. Fogtown incorporates many of those flavors into its small-batch beer. From two separate locations the brewers turn out lagers and ales brewed with Maine-grown malt, as well as Maine-grown hops, giving a taste of the Pine Tree State to each pint.

SPICY TAPENADE RAGU WITH LINGUINE

Coppertail Brewing Co.

TAMPA, FLORIDA

The Pairing: Belgian-Style Strong Ale

There is a satisfaction that comes with having a pot of sauce bubbling on the stove in the hours leading to dinner. And as the house fills with its alluring aromas, the anticipation builds. This savory sauce incorporates Mediterranean flavors but pairs beautifully with Belgian-style strong ales, especially ones with prominent fruity esters, a touch of spice, and a well-balanced malt backbone.

Serves 4 to 6

3 Tbsp extra-virgin olive oil
¼ cup salt-packed capers, rinsed
8 sun-dried tomatoes in oil, chopped
8 garlic cloves, smashed and peeled
6 oil-packed anchovy fillets, chopped
4 red Fresno chiles, seeded and chopped
4 gherkins, chopped
2 red onions, chopped
One 28 oz can whole peeled tomatoes
1½ cups Dunkel or Oktoberfest lager
¾ cup Kalamata olives, pitted and halved
Kosher salt and freshly ground black pepper
1 lb linguine or other long thin pasta
8 caper berries, for serving
2 Tbsp finely chopped fresh flat-leaf parsley, for serving

In a large saucepan, heat the olive oil over medium-high heat. Add the capers, sun-dried tomatoes, garlic, anchovies, chiles, gherkins, and red onions and cook, stirring occasionally, for 20 minutes, or until browned. Add the canned tomatoes and their juices and the beer, turn the heat to high, and bring to a boil. Turn the heat to medium-low and simmer, uncovered and stirring occasionally, for about 1½ hours, or until the sauce thickens. Transfer the sauce to a blender and purée until smooth. Return the sauce to the pan, stir in the olives, and season with salt and pepper. Keep warm over low heat.

Bring a large pot of salted water to a boil. Add the linguine and cook for 8 to 10 minutes, or until al dente. Drain the linguine, reserving some of the pasta water. Add the linguine to the sauce and stir to combine, stirring in a little pasta water, if desired, to loosen the sauce. Divide the linguine and sauce among plates or bowls, sprinkle with caper berries and parsley, and serve.

Coppertail Brewing Co.

Drawing inspiration from the flavors of Florida, but with an eye toward the world, Coppertail Brewing has spent the last decade creating reliably tasty beers and serving them up to thirsty patrons in their taproom and throughout the southern part of the Sunshine State. From their flagship porter and tripel to seasonal releases that showcase local ingredients and creativity, this brewery, named after a mythical sea monster (albeit one named by the owners' then-5-year-old daughter), never leaves you dry.

GRILLED TOFU WITH FRUITY KOREAN BARBECUE SAUCE

Serves 4

TOFU

1 lb extra-firm tofu
2 to 4 Tbsp paprika
2 to 4 Tbsp garlic powder
2 Tbsp kosher salt
1½ Tbsp freshly ground
    black pepper
1 cup shredded cabbage
    (about 4 oz)
¼ cup finely chopped
    fresh cilantro
Juice of ½ lime

SAUCE

1 Tbsp sesame oil
1 Tbsp freshly grated ginger
2 garlic cloves, minced
1 cup light brown sugar
¾ cup tamari
½ cup pineapple juice
⅓ cup fresh lime juice
⅓ cup gochugaru
¼ cup rice vinegar
1 Tbsp sambal oelek
2 Tbsp cornstarch

Aslan Brewing Co.
BELLINGHAM, WASHINGTON

The Pairing: Saison

Aslan Brewing's twist on Korean barbecue sauce has fruity undertones thanks to the addition of lime and pineapple juice, while the more traditional gochugaru (Korean red pepper powder) and brown sugar maintain its powerful sweet and spicy flavor. Using tamari and tofu keeps the recipe gluten-free and vegan. Gochugaru and sambal oelek chili paste can be found in the international section of many grocery stores. Pair with a classic saison like Aslan's Frances Farmer.

To make the tofu: Drain the tofu, pat it dry, and cut into three thin sheets along the horizontal axis.

In a small bowl, combine the paprika, garlic powder, salt, and pepper, adding more or less paprika and garlic powder, depending on your preference. Rub the spice mixture liberally on the tofu then put the tofu on a plate, cover, and refrigerate overnight or for at least 2 hours.

To make the sauce: In a large sauce pan, combine the sesame oil, ginger, and garlic over medium heat and cook, stirring occasionally, for 2 minutes. Add the brown sugar, tamari, pineapple juice, lime juice, gochugaru, rice vinegar, and sambal oelek. Turn the heat to high and bring to a boil.

In a small bowl, whisk the cornstarch with 2 Tbsp of water to make a slurry. Add to the sauce and simmer for 1 minute. Transfer the sauce to a bowl and refrigerate for 10 minutes to cool.

Heat a grill to 375°F. Put the marinated tofu directly on the grill grates, generously brush the sauce on the top, and grill for 5 minutes. Flip the tofu, brush the cooked side with sauce, and grill for 4 to 5 more minutes, or until the tofu is crispy. Arrange the shredded cabbage on a plate and put the tofu on top. Finish with cilantro and a squeeze of lime juice and serve immediately.

Aslan Brewing Co.

The founders of Aslan, named after the king of the jungle (aslan means "lion" in Turkish), have made it the company's mission to be benevolent to the local ecosystem. From working with other small, local companies to increasing the quality of life for their employees and community, Aslan puts the planet and its citizens before profit.

SPICE-RUBBED PORK BLADE STEAKS WITH BARBECUE SAUCE

Serves 4

BARBECUE SAUCE

2 cups ketchup

1 cup apple cider vinegar

¾ cup vegetable oil

1 onion, coarsely chopped

2 Tbsp Worcestershire sauce

2 Tbsp dried mustard powder

2 tsp freshly ground
   black pepper

BARBECUE RUB

1 tsp whole cumin seed

1 tsp whole fennel seed

1 Tbsp kosher salt

1 Tbsp smoked paprika

1 Tbsp dark brown sugar

1 tsp dry mustard

1 tsp garlic powder

1 tsp freshly ground
   black pepper

STEAKS

4 pork blade (shoulder)
   steaks, each ¾ to
   1 in thick

Alesong Brewing & Blending

EUGENE, OREGON

The Pairing: Dry-Hopped Brettanomyces Saison

Pork shoulder steaks have an intense meaty flavor that is well complemented by a hoppy, earthy, spicy saison, like Alesong's Touch of Brett. Brewer Matt Van Wyk points out that these steaks, known as either blade steaks or shoulder steaks, are NOT pork chops. You may find them at the grocery store, but if not, a trip to the local butcher might be in order. Alternatively, you can cut your own steaks from a shoulder roast. For a complete meal, serve these steaks with roasted fingerling potatoes and a kale and Parmesan salad. Note that the sauce can be made in advance and is great with other dishes, such as kale salad with Parmesan, roasted potatoes, or grilled vegetables.

To make the sauce: In a large pot, bring the ketchup, vinegar, vegetable oil, onion, Worcestershire sauce, mustard powder, and pepper to a simmer over medium heat. Continue simmering, stirring occasionally, for about 1 hour, or until thick. Remove from the heat and let cool then put in a tightly covered container and refrigerate until ready to use.

To make the dry rub: Heat a cast-iron skillet or other frying pan over medium-high heat and toast the cumin and fennel seeds for 4 to 5 minutes, or until fragrant and starting to brown. Remove from the heat and allow to cool then use a spice grinder to grind them into a powder. Put the ground spices in a small bowl, add the salt, paprika, brown sugar, dry mustard, garlic powder, and pepper, and stir to combine.

To make the steaks: Pat the steaks dry with a paper towel and then rub all over with the spice mixture. Refrigerate for at least 1 hour or up to 1 day. Remove the steaks from the refrigerator at least 20 minutes before cooking.

Heat a gas grill to high or get a charcoal grill extremely hot. Put the steaks directly on the grates, generously brush the top with barbecue sauce, and grill for 5 minutes. Flip the steaks, brush the cooked side with barbecue sauce, and grill for about 4 more minutes, or until the internal temperature reaches 145°F. Let rest for 5 minutes then serve with extra barbecue sauce on the side.

Alesong Brewing & Blending

From his small brewery in Oregon's wine country, brewer Matt Van Wyk and his team are making beers that have long inspired them. The goal of Alesong is to focus on small batches, brewing with locally harvested fruits when possible and letting the flavors spend time in barrels until they unfold into memorable beer experiences. "We like to say that our beers are influenced by the terroir of the ingredients we use," says Van Wyk. One taste and you'll agree.

CHOCOLATE ZUCCHINI CAKE

The Pairing: Lambic

A delicious way to sneak in extra vegetables, this decadent dessert features both chocolate ganache and cream cheese frosting. But the real benefit of the zucchini is how moist the cake turns out. Pair it with a fruit lambic, such as kriek or pêche, which will complement the chocolate—and fruit is healthy, too, right?

To make the cake: Preheat the oven to 350°F. Butter and flour two 9 in round cake pans.

In a medium bowl, whisk together the flour, granulated sugar, brown sugar, cocoa powder, baking soda, baking powder, cinnamon, salt, and nutmeg. Add the eggs and butter and mix into a batter. Add the zucchini and chocolate chips and fold until evenly distributed. Divide the batter between the prepared pans and bake for 50 to 60 minutes, or until a knife inserted in the center comes out clean. Let the cakes cool on a wire rack for 10 minutes then carefully remove from the pans to cool completely.

To make the ganache: Put the chocolate chips in a medium heatproof bowl. In a small saucepan, bring the cream to a gentle simmer over medium heat. Pour the heated cream over the chocolate chips, add the sugar and amaretto and whisk until smooth. Allow the ganache to cool slightly then pour on top of the cakes, starting in the center and spreading it outwards and over the sides. Then stack the cakes and allow to set for 2 to 4 hours.

To make the frosting: In medium bowl, beat together the cream cheese and butter until smooth. Slowly add the confectioners' sugar and vanilla, beating until fully incorporated. Immediately frost the cake, cut into slices, and serve.

Serves 8

CAKE
3 cups all-purpose flour
1½ cups granulated sugar
1½ cups light brown sugar
1 cup unsweetened cocoa
    power
1 Tbsp baking soda
1½ tsp baking powder
1½ tsp ground cinnamon
¾ tsp fine sea salt
½ tsp ground nutmeg
6 large eggs
1 cup plus 2 Tbsp
    (2¼ sticks) butter,
    at room temperature
5 zucchini, grated with excess
    moisture removed
6 oz semisweet chocolate
    chips

GANACHE
18 oz semisweet chocolate
    chips
2 cups heavy cream
¼ cup granulated sugar
4 tsp amaretto liqueur

FROSTING
Two 8 oz packages cream
    cheese, at room
    temperature
½ cup (1 stick) unsalted
    butter, at room
    temperature
3 cups sifted confectioners'
    sugar

Dark Ales

A beer's color is measured by the standard reference method, and its color is derived from malt. The darker the malt, the more a roasted character is typically present in the flavor and aromas of a beer. This often lends tastes of coffee or chocolate, even when those ingredients aren't added.

Dark ales get an overall bad rap. Drinkers unfamiliar with the flavors will say they are too bold, assertive, or heavy, without giving them a proper try. Yet many of these same drinkers also enjoy cups of coffee in the morning.

Irish stout is the most well-known style of dark ale, and this is thanks to Guinness, the Irish brewer that for more than 300 years has been turning out a black ale that is light in body but big on roasted flavor. The nitrogenated pour, only developed in the 1950s, is iconic and creates that famous cascading gas effect in the glass, complete with a thick and creamy white cake of foam on top. Guinness is made with roasted barley and black malt, which impart cocoa and java flavors.

Yet there is more to dark ales than just the Irish stout, and exploring the category can reveal pleasing flavors that pair well with a variety of foods, not just desserts. Stouts, porters, and brown ales, for instance, are great with roasted and grilled meats and vegetables.

Compared to stouts, porters are more rounded and soft, with a more pronounced chocolate character. Brown ales are usually drier with a sweeter malt flavor and light fruity notes. Both are ideal pairings for a simple grilled burger. The char on the meat, along with the caramelization of the fats, complement the roasted characteristics and sweetness of the beer.

The milk stout, sometimes called sweet stout or cream stout, has long been a staple in brewing. As the name suggests, it has lactose added, and the milk sugar adds a creamy mouthfeel to the beer, along with a dose of sweetness that perfectly complements its roasted coffee, chocolate, and toast flavors. As modern beer trends push dark ales like the milk stout toward the sweeter end of the spectrum, a new style has emerged: the pastry stout. With these beers, brewers attempt to mimic well-known desserts, from German chocolate cake to cinnamon rolls to fruit pies, in beer form. It has breathed new life into milk stouts, and brewers are using it to reach into the sugary stratosphere.

Dark ales are also ideally suited for the addition of actual coffee, as well as for barrel aging. Many brewers work with local coffee roasters to find just the right blend to complement a stout or porter, while distilleries, especially bourbon makers, are happy to sell used barrels to breweries that fill the wood with strong stouts. Barrel-aged beers, big on whisky and vanilla flavors, are often released for special occasions. Barleywines, boozy dark ales with aromas and flavors of butterscotch and caramel, along with fig, raisins, and dried stone fruits like cherry, are particularly well suited for barrel aging.

Stouts and oysters make a great pairing (although Chef Arlin Smith stands by tripel as the best pairing, see page 62) with a bit of roast in the beer complementing the saltiness of the shellfish. There are even some breweries that make stouts brewed with oyster liquor or steeped on shells.

Exploring the dark side of ales will result in delightful flavors that can match most meals.

COFFEE PORTER PANCAKES WITH CINNAMON APPLES

Serves 6 to 8

APPLES

4 Granny Smith apples, peeled, cored, and cut into ⅛ in slices
Juice of 1 lemon
½ cup granulated sugar
1 tsp ground cinnamon
1 Tbsp unsalted butter

PANCAKES

1½ cups all-purpose flour
1 Tbsp granulated sugar
2 tsp baking powder
1 tsp baking soda
1 tsp ground cinnamon
½ tsp fine sea salt
1¼ cups coffee porter
¼ cup molasses
3 Tbsp unsalted butter, melted
1 tsp pure vanilla extract

The Pairing: Coffee Porter or Stout

Putting coffee porter in pancake batter, as well as in your mug, adds to the warming sensation needed as a nip of chill hits the autumn air. These are a hearty treat to enjoy at home, especially after a trip to the local apple orchard. In lieu of coffee porter, you can use a coffee-infused stout.

To make the apples: In a large bowl, toss the apple slices with the lemon juice, sugar, and cinnamon.

In a large sauté pan or skillet, melt the butter over medium heat. Add the apple mixture and cook, stirring often, for about 8 minutes, or until the apples are tender. Remove from the heat, set aside, and keep warm.

To make the pancakes: In a medium bowl, sift together the flour, sugar, baking powder, baking soda, cinnamon, and salt. Add the beer, molasses, melted butter, and vanilla and whisk until fully combined.

Generously butter a large skillet and place over medium heat. Ladle enough batter into the hot pan to create a 6 in diameter pancake and cook for 2 to 3 minutes, or until bubbles form and pop on the top. Flip the pancake and cook for 2 more minutes, or until the center is firm. Repeat to cook more pancakes, adding more butter to the pan as needed.

Serve immediately with cinnamon apples and a coffee porter.

WARM FARRO, MUSHROOM, AND ROMANESCO SALAD WITH ROASTED POBLANO SAUCE

Serves 4 to 6

SAUCE

2 fire-roasted poblano
    peppers, peeled and
    deseeded
1 small bunch fresh cilantro
    leaves
1 cup arugula, blanched
⅓ cup pistachios, toasted
4 garlic cloves
Juice of 1 lime
1 Tbsp white wine vinegar
1 tsp fine sea salt
¾ cup extra-virgin olive oil
Freshly ground black pepper

SALAD

2 cups farro
1 cup oyster mushrooms,
    trimmed and roughly
    chopped
1 cup shiitake mushrooms,
    trimmed and roughly
    chopped
1 Tbsp plus 2 tsp extra-virgin
    olive oil

continues ↗

Good Word Brewing & Public House

DULUTH, GEORGIA

The Pairing: Imperial Stout

Though it comes together quickly, this warm salad, from the brewery's kitchen, has a depth of flavor that will excite the taste buds. An imperial stout might seem heavy, but the peppers complement the beer's roast character. The beer also boosts the farro's nuttiness, bringing additional layers to a dish that can be enjoyed as a side or a main. While you can roast poblanos at home—use the broiler or the flame on a gas stove— they can also be purchased in jars.

To make the sauce: In a food processor, combine the roasted poblanos, cilantro, arugula, pistachios, garlic, lime juice, white wine vinegar, salt, and 2 Tbsp of water. Blend until fully combined. With the processor on, gradually add the olive oil, blending until fully incorporated. Season with salt and pepper. Set aside.

To make the salad: Preheat the oven to 375°F.

Bring a medium saucepan of salted water to boil over medium heat. Add the farro and boil for 20 to 25 minutes, or until tender. Drain the farro then spread it on a baking sheet to cool.

Spread the mushrooms and cauliflower on a clean baking sheet, toss with 2 tsp of the olive oil, and season with salt and pepper. Bake for 10 to 15 minutes, or until tender.

Good Word Brewing & Public House
The word "community" gets tossed around a lot when it comes to beer, but at this small public house in Georgia, it's a way of life and helps bring people together over a shared passion and a desire for good food and drink. While Good Word has an expansive and eclectic tap list and kitchen, the brewery has excelled at small batch lagers, often done as collaborations with other brewers and the occasional writer, like the prolific Stan Hieronymus.

Fine sea salt and freshly
    ground black pepper
½ head Romanesco
    cauliflower or regular
    cauliflower, cut into florets
2 cups chopped kale
1 Tbsp white wine vinegar
2 cups baby arugula
½ cup breadcrumbs, toasted
½ cup pickled onions

When ready to serve, in a large sauté pan, heat the remaining 1 Tbsp of olive oil over medium heat. Add the mushrooms and cauliflower and cook, stirring, just until warmed through. Add the farro and kale and cook, stirring, until the kale has started to wilt and the farro is warming up and starting to toast in the oil. Remove from the heat, add the vinegar, and stir to incorporate. Transfer to a large bowl, add the baby arugula and roasted poblano sauce, and toss to combine. Sprinkle with the toasted breadcrumbs and pickled onions and serve.

BAKED BEER BEANS

Serves 4

4 oz bacon, diced

½ red bell pepper, diced

½ yellow onion, diced

¾ cup diced precooked sausage links

One 16 oz can pinto beans, drained and rinsed

¾ cup oatmeal stout or coffee stout, such as Bissell Brothers Umbra or First Crack, plus additional as needed

¼ cup apple juice, plus additional as needed

⅛ cup brown sugar

¼ chipotle chile in adobo sauce, chopped

¼ tsp chili powder

¼ tsp Worcestershire sauce

¼ tsp yellow mustard

¼ tsp onion powder

¼ tsp smoked paprika

¼ tsp cumin

⅛ tsp garlic powder

⅛ tsp freshly ground black pepper

Bissell Brothers

PORTLAND, MAINE

The Pairing: Brown Ale

A staple of any proper summer cookout, these baked beans can be made with an oatmeal stout or a coffee stout, which adds some extra roasted flavors to the final dish. A cold glass of brown ale nearby will complement the spices and meatiness of the beans as well as other dishes coming off the grill.

Line a plate with a paper towel.

In a large Dutch oven or other heavy pot, cook the bacon over medium heat for about 7 minutes, or until crispy and brown. Transfer the bacon to the paper towel–lined plate to drain. Pour off all but 2 Tbsp of the fat in the Dutch oven and reserve for another use. Add the bell pepper, onion, and sausage and cook, stirring occasionally, for about 5 minutes, or until the peppers are soft and the onions are translucent. Add the beans, beer, apple juice, brown sugar, chipotle chile, chili powder, Worcestershire sauce, yellow mustard, onion powder, paprika, cumin, garlic powder, and pepper and stir well to combine. Bring to a simmer and then turn the heat to low, cover, and cook, adding more beer or apple juice if the mixture gets too dry, for 2 to 3 hours, or until the sauce is thick. Serve immediately.

Bissell Brothers

When beer fans visit Portland, Maine, this brewery is often at the top of their list. And for good reason. When it opened in 2011, in a small industrial space across the street from the well-established Allagash Brewing Company, the Bissell Brothers—Peter and Noah—began experimenting with New England–style IPAs. Their hazy concoctions helped usher in a phenomenon that took the beer world by storm. Today, they are in a larger facility, as well as a satellite location in the northern part of the state, and they continue to make a diverse array of styles, including brown ales, that seek to forge new ground.

SHRIMP, SAUSAGE, AND GRITS

Serves 4

HERB BUTTER

½ cup (1 stick) unsalted
   butter, at room
   temperature
¼ cup hot sauce, such
   as Tabasco
Juice of 1 lemon
2 garlic cloves, minced
2 Tbsp chopped fresh flat-
   leaf parsley
1 Tbsp chopped fresh thyme
Fine sea salt and freshly
   ground black pepper

**SHRIMP, SAUSAGE,
AND GRITS**

1 lb corn grits
4 oz Cheddar cheese,
   shredded
2 lbs fresh shrimp, peeled
   and deveined
1 Tbsp paprika
1 Tbsp cayenne pepper
1 tsp ground cumin
1 lb fresh andouille sausage,
   cut into coins
4 scallions, chopped

Roadhouse Pub & Eatery

JACKSON HOLE, WYOMING

The Pairing: Sweet Potato Porter

With sautéed shrimp, smoked andouille sausage, Cheddar cheese grits, and Tabasco butter, this is a savory and hearty meal that sticks to the ribs and has a wonderful combination of flavors that range from tangy to spicy, sweet to salty. An earthy porter, like Roadhouse's Sweet Potato Porter, is an unexpected pairing, but its roast character stands up to the sausage, while its light sweetness complements the sausage and grits. Grits are a personal dish for so many people that it's best to follow your own family recipe or the instructions on the package for best results.

To make the herb butter: In a small bowl, combine the butter, hot sauce, lemon juice, garlic, parsley, and thyme and mash with a fork until fully combined. Season with salt and pepper. Transfer the butter to a piece of wax paper and roll the paper around the butter to create a log shape. Secure the paper with tape or string and refrigerate for at least 1 hour or overnight.

To make the shrimp, sausage, and grits: Make the grits according to your family recipe or the package instructions. When finished, add the cheese and stir until melted and incorporated. Keep warm.

In a large bowl, combine the shrimp, paprika, cayenne pepper, and cumin and toss to combine.

In a large sauté pan or skillet, melt 2 Tbsp of the herb butter over medium heat. Add the sausage and cook, turning occasionally, for 5 minutes, or until starting to brown. Add another 2 Tbsp of the herb butter and when melted, add the shrimp and cook, stirring, for 3 to 5 minutes, or until the shrimp turn pink. Refrigerate the rest of the herb butter and reserve for a later use.

Spoon the grits onto a serving plate and top with the sausage and shrimp. Sprinkle with the scallions and serve immediately.

Roadhouse Pub & Eatery

There are breweries that make a serious impression in the glass, and then, when you dig a little deeper, also have a cool story to tell. That's Roadhouse Brewing. Based in Jackson Hole, Wyoming, they could have simply catered to the tourists and locals, but choose to bust onto the larger scene, with their hop-forward ales, brewed with hops harvested from neighboring Idaho, and pilsners that are crisp and refreshing, and perfect after a long day out in nature, be it skiing or fly fishing.

LONG-SIMMER WEEKEND CHILI

Serves 12

2 Tbsp vegetable oil

5 lbs beef chuck roast, cut
   into 1 in cubes

2 lbs ground turkey

1 large yellow onion, minced

6 garlic cloves, minced

1 large carrot, minced

Four 14 oz cans diced
   tomatoes

6 chipotle chiles in adobo,
   minced

1 Tbsp ground cumin

1 Tbsp dried thyme

Fine sea salt and freshly
   ground black pepper

3 cups lager or stout

Sour cream, for serving

Shredded Cheddar cheese,
   for serving

Chopped scallions, for serving

Atlas Brew Works

WASHINGTON, D.C.

The Pairing: Rye Stout

Here's a recipe for a crowd. It comes from the kitchen of Daniel Vilarrubi, the head brewer at Atlas Brew Works, who recommends starting early in the morning and allowing the chili to simmer all day. This adds depth to the ingredients and fills the house with aromas that build anticipation for dinner. Serve this hearty beef and turkey chili topped with sour cream, Cheddar cheese, and scallions and paired with a rye stout like Atlas Brew Works' Silent Neighbor, which has both roast character and a touch of spice to complement the smokiness of the chipotle.

In a large Dutch oven or other heavy pot, heat the vegetable oil over medium-high heat. Working in batches, sear the chuck roast, turning, for about 2 minutes per side, or until browned all over. Transfer to a large bowl. Add the ground turkey to the pot and cook, breaking it up with a wooden spoon, for about 10 minutes, or until golden. Add to the bowl with the beef and set aside.

Add the onion to the pot and cook over low heat, stirring to coat the onion in the oil and scraping up any bits of browned meat from the bottom of the pot, for about 7 minutes, or until the onions are translucent. Add the garlic and carrot and cook, stirring frequently, for 3 minutes. Return the beef and turkey to the pot, add the tomatoes and their juices and the chipotle chiles and adobo, and stir to combine. Turn the heat to medium and bring to a simmer. Add the cumin and thyme and season with salt and pepper. Turn the heat to low and cook for 6 hours, adding lager or stout as needed to keep the chili from drying out. Serve topped with sour cream, Cheddar cheese, and scallions.

Atlas Brew Works

When Justin Cox, originally from Tennessee, decided to leave his government job in Washington, DC, behind, he started a brewery. There, he figured, he could do good work, serve people, and make a positive impact. Now, with two locations in the capital and a crew turning out stellar beer of all kinds, Atlas Brew Works is helping establish the District as a beer destination.

SHORT RIBS RELLENOS

Serves 6

4 lbs whole-slab beef
    short ribs
1 cup Irish stout or porter
2 cups chicken or beef stock
3 celery stalks, peeled
    and diced
2 garlic cloves, minced
1 medium onion, diced
2 Tbsp tomato paste
2 Tbsp finely chopped
    fresh thyme
Fine sea salt and freshly
    ground black pepper
6 large poblano peppers
1½ cups all-purpose flour
1 cup seltzer water or
    club soda
¼ cup cornstarch
1 large egg, beaten
2 cups vegetable oil,
    for frying

By All Means Brew Lab
BILLINGS, MONTANA

The Pairing: Irish Stout

Stuffed poblano peppers are easy to make and look great on the plate—they'll impress your guests with both presentation and flavor. Brewer Travis Zeilstra suggests pairing this dish with an Irish stout. The roasted dry notes of the malt will play really nicely with the short ribs, while the beer's smooth body will combat some of the spice.

Preheat the oven to 350°F.

Heat a large Dutch oven or other heavy pot over medium-high heat. Add the short ribs and sear, turning as needed, for about 5 minutes, or until both sides have a crust. Add the beer and deglaze the pan, using a wooden spoon to scrape any browned bits off the bottom. Add the stock, celery, garlic, onion, tomato paste, and thyme. Stir to combine, season with salt and pepper, and cover. Place the pan in the oven and braise for 3 hours, or until the meat is tender and has separated from the bone.

Transfer the meat to a cutting board and allow to cool slightly then use forks to shred it into small pieces, removing any bones. Return the meat to the Dutch oven and bring to a simmer over medium-low heat. Continue simmering for about 30 minutes, or until reduced by half. Keep warm.

Meanwhile, set a rack in the upper third of the oven and turn on the broiler.

Place the poblano peppers on a baking sheet and broil for 4 minutes. Turn the peppers over and continue broiling, turning every minute, for about 6 minutes, or until starting to char and blister. Let the peppers cool to room temperature then peel the skins and rinse under cool water.

Make a lengthwise slit in the peppers and remove the seeds. Fill each pepper with the shredded short rib.

In a large bowl, whisk together 1 cup of the flour, the seltzer water, cornstarch, egg, and 1 Tbsp of salt.

Fill a large Dutch oven, deep pot, or deep fryer with 2 in of the vegetable oil and heat to 350°F on a thermometer. Line a baking sheet with paper towels.

By All Means Brew Lab
*Think of By All Means as
more of a laboratory than
a brewery. Food and beer
teams work to unlock new
processes and flavors, and
to create recipes that stand
out on their own, as well as
together. With a rotating
lineup of beers, in styles like
pale ale, sour, and lager,
the brewers use different
hops and different malts to
create memorable flavor
combinations in the glass.*

Place the remaining ½ cup of flour in a shallow bowl. Dip each stuffed pepper in the batter, shaking off any excess, then dredge in the flour. Working in batches, fry the peppers, turning as needed, for 4 to 6 minutes, or until golden brown. Transfer the peppers to the paper towel–lined baking sheet. Fry the remaining peppers, adjusting the heat as needed to keep the oil at 350°F. Serve immediately topped with the sauce the meat was cooked in.

COFFEE- AND CHILI-RUBBED VENISON LOIN WITH ROMESCO SAUCE

Serves 6 to 8

ROMESCO SAUCE

2 large tomatoes, quartered

1 shallot, sliced

2 Tbsp sherry vinegar

1 Tbsp plus ½ cup extra-virgin
    olive oil

Kosher salt and freshly ground
    black pepper

1 large bell pepper, quartered
    and seeded

½ cup toasted almonds

½ cup toasted crumbled
    cornbread

VENISON

¾ cup finely ground
    coffee beans

½ cup chili powder

½ tsp garlic powder

5 lbs venison loin

Kosher salt and freshly ground
    black pepper

Sorghum or maple syrup,
    for brushing

Blackberry Farm Brewery

MARYVILLE, TENNESSEE

The Pairing: American Stout

The rub in this recipe, from the kitchens of the famed Blackberry Farm, is a great accompaniment to grilled or poached meats and vegetables and the romesco, a purée of peppers and tomato, can also be used as a spread on crackers. Pair the venison with a roast-forward American stout with noticeable hops. The coffee and chocolate notes in the beer will accent the rub, and the spicy, earthy hops will complement the sauce.

To make the romesco sauce: Preheat the oven to 375°F.

In a baking dish large enough to fit the tomatoes, toss the tomatoes and shallots with the sherry and 1 Tbsp of olive oil. Season with salt and pepper and roast for about 20 minutes, or until the tomatoes and shallots are soft.

While the tomatoes are roasting, roast the bell pepper quarters on a hot grill, over the flame of a gas burner, or under a broiler for about 4 minutes, or until starting to soften and char but not burn, remove from oven, allow to cool, and peel.

Transfer the tomatoes, shallots, and any liquid from the baking dish to a blender. Add the bell pepper, almonds, and cornbread and purée until broken apart. With the blender on, gradually add the remaining ½ cup of olive oil and blend until the sauce is smooth. Season with salt and sherry vinegar.

Blackberry Farm Brewery
The saying at Blackberry Farm Brewery is that farm roots run deep, and that is evidenced in the wide array of beers coming out of this mountain farm in western Tennessee. The brewery has created some of the most flavorful saisons in the country that are nearly bottomless in their depth. Part of a larger hospitality group that includes a restaurant and hotel, it continually reaches the highest levels of culinary and hospitality achievement. The brewery's commitment to quality and community is evident in every pint.

To make the venison: Preheat the oven to 275°F.

In a small bowl, whisk together the coffee, chili powder, and garlic powder. Season the meat with salt and pepper. Generously rub the coffee mixture all over the meat, making sure to cover it on all sides. Let stand at room temperature for 20 minutes, so the coffee can start to dissolve.

Heat a grill pan or skillet over medium-high heat until lightly smoking. Add the venison and sear, turning as needed, for about 5 minutes, or until a dark chestnut color on all sides. Brush the sorghum syrup all over the venison then transfer to the oven and continue cooking for about 40 to 60 minutes, or until the meat reaches 125°F on a thermometer. Transfer the venison to a cutting board and let rest for 5 minutes. Slice the venison and serve topped with the romesco sauce.

CITRUS CHEESECAKE

Serves 8 to 12

1¼ cups graham cracker
   crumbs

½ cup (1 stick) unsalted
   butter, melted

Four 8 oz packages cream
   cheese, at room
   temperature

1 cup sour cream

1 cup granulated sugar

¾ cup wheat beer

2 large eggs

½ Tbsp freshly grated
   lemon zest

½ tsp pure vanilla extract

1 cup fresh orange juice

1 cup light brown sugar

2 Tbsp orange-flavored
   liqueur, such as Grand
   Marnier

The Pairing: Barleywine

Cheesecake can be a labor-intensive undertaking, but the hard work is worth it. The same is true with the creation of a barleywine. A full-bodied boozy barley with undertones of stone fruit, caramel, and toffee matches well with this rich, citrus-forward cake, creating a decadent dessert pairing for celebrations or any old Tuesday night.

In a medium bowl, stir together the graham crackers and melted butter until the crumbs are evenly moistened. Press the graham cracker mixture evenly into the bottom and up the sides of a 10 in or smaller nonstick springform pan. Refrigerate for 5 to 10 minutes to firm.

Preheat the oven to 325°F.

In the bowl of a stand mixer fitted with the paddle attachment or using a handheld mixer, beat the cream cheese until smooth. Add the sour cream, sugar, beer, eggs, lemon zest, and vanilla and continue beating until well incorporated and creamy. Pour into the chilled crust and bake for 40 to 45 minutes—the cheesecake should still be a little soft in the middle and not cracked. Set on a wire rack and let cool for 15 to 20 minutes at room temperature then loosely cover the pan and refrigerate for 4 hours.

Meanwhile, in a small saucepan, bring the orange juice, brown sugar, and liqueur to a gentle boil over medium-high heat. Continue gently boiling for 20 to 30 minutes, or until the sauce is thick. Remove from the heat and let cool.

Remove the sides of the springform pan then slice the cheesecake, drizzle with the orange sauce, and serve.

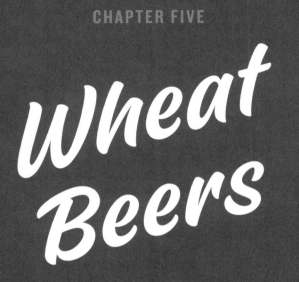

Wheat Beers

Haze is in fashion these days thanks to a new breed of IPAs. In the past, when something was served cloudy or yeast-forward, it was usually a wheat beer. These workhorses of the beer world don't always get the love they deserve from large numbers of beer drinkers, but attention should be paid by all.

As the name suggests, wheat is a primary ingredient in wheat beer. This makes these beers heartier and more earthy, but this style is actually quite versatile and can be a lot of fun to pair with food. While wheat in the grain bill is the unifying ingredient in the category, it is the yeast strains and adjuncts like spices and fruits that help divide wheat beers into categories. The hefeweizen has aromas of banana and clove, while the witbier is often softer, with a touch of spice. These are beers that can be enjoyed both at a summer picnic and by a fireplace in winter. Often, these two wheat beer styles are served with a lemon wedge or orange slice.

As wheat beers become better known by a new generation of drinkers, some brewers have dusted off recipes for forgotten styles like grisette, a low abv beer that is usually citrus or fruit-forward without the addition of actual produce.

Many brewers have taken the farmhouse tradition for making wheat beers and begun working with local maltsters (malt makers) and hop growers, as well as harvesting local yeast, to create a true sense of place in a bottle. No matter where wheat beers are made, however, they deserve to be in your glass.

A versatile beer style calls for diversity in food. Paired with everything from fresh seafood that gets a pop from lemon to homemade bread with herbed compound butter to lamb shanks and stews, the heartiness of this beer style adds effervescence and a little bit of body to a meal.

SHAKSHUKA

Serves 2 to 4

2 Tbsp olive oil

1 large white onion,
    finely diced

½ jalapeño or Fresno pepper,
    seeded and finely diced

1 large red bell pepper,
    finely chopped

4 tomatoes, diced

3 Tbsp tomato paste

Fine sea salt and freshly
    ground black pepper

6 large eggs

4 to 5 scallions, chopped,
    for serving

3 to 4 oz crumbled feta, for
    serving

Pita or other bread, for serving

The Pairing: Belgian Witbier

Shakshuka is a North African and Middle Eastern meal that is perfect for breaking up the same old breakfast rut but also delightful later in the day. Brewer Amit Ram shared this recipe and says that while you would traditionally serve shakshuka on or with pita, you can also use fresh challah or any kind of country loaf or sourdough. For a little more oomph, Ram suggests a smear of hummus or harissa on the bread. Pair this spicy egg-and-tomato dish with a Belgian witbier that has a soft wheat-forward body and some spice to complement the heat from the peppers and the acidity from the tomatoes.

In a large skillet, heat the olive oil over medium heat until shimmering. Add the onion and cook, stirring occasionally, for about 4 minutes, or until glossy. Add the jalapeño and bell pepper and cook, stirring, for 2 minutes, or until softened. Add the tomatoes and bring to a simmer. Continue simmering for 10 minutes, or until reduced to a sauce-like consistency. Add the tomato paste and season with salt and pepper. Turn the heat to low then create cavities in the sauce and add the eggs, one at a time and spaced apart from each other. Cover the pan and cook for about 5 minutes, or until the egg whites are set and the yolk is still runny, or to your desired level of doneness. Sprinkle with scallions and feta and serve immediately with pita or bread.

CHICKEN LIVER MOUSSE WITH RED ONION MARMALADE

Serves 6 to 8

RED ONION MARMALADE

¼ cup canola oil

4 large red onions, diced

1½ cups red wine

2 cups dark brown sugar

1 cup balsamic vinegar

10 sprigs fresh thyme

1 tsp ground allspice

1 Tbsp apple pectin

Kosher salt

CHICKEN LIVER MOUSSE

1 lb chicken livers, cleaned, rinsed, and patted dry

Kosher salt and freshly ground black pepper

2 cups heavy cream

2 cups (4 sticks) unsalted butter, at room temperature, cut into small pieces

3 shallots, roughly chopped

6 garlic cloves, roughly chopped

½ cup cognac or brandy

½ cup dark brown sugar

2 Tbsp fresh oregano

2 Tbsp fresh thyme

Fair State Brewing Cooperative

MINNEAPOLIS, MINNESOTA

The Pairing: Lichtenhainer

Ideal as a shared plate or pre-dinner snack, this mousse is packed with fresh herbal and deep boozy flavors. The red onion marmalade is a versatile and easy to make spread that also goes well smeared across toasted baguettes or rolls at dinner. It needs to chill for a few hours, so plan to make that in advance of the mousse. Pair with a lichtenhainer, a delicate smoked wheat beer that will brighten the pickled onion and add depth to the chicken liver.

To make the red onion marmalade: In the bottom of a large Dutch oven or other heavy pot, heat a thin layer of canola oil over medium heat. Add the red onions and cook, stirring frequently, for 12 minutes, or until translucent. Add the red wine and bring to a simmer. Continue simmering for about 20 minutes, or until reduced by half. Add the brown sugar, balsamic vinegar, thyme, and allspice and stir well to combine. Return to a simmer and continue simmering for about 40 minutes, or until the liquid is nearly evaporated. Slowly whisk in the pectin and season with salt. When the liquid thinly coats the back of a spoon, cover and simmer for 10 minutes. Transfer the marmalade to a serving bowl, cover, and refrigerate for 3 to 4 hours.

To make the chicken liver mousse: Season the chicken livers with salt and pepper and set aside.

In a medium pot, bring the heavy cream to a boil over high heat then immediately turn the heat to low and simmer the cream. Season with salt. Gradually add 1 cup (2 sticks) of the butter, 1 Tbsp at a time, whisking until well incorporated.

Fair State Brewing Cooperative

This community-minded brewery works to make sure the company and its beers are doing right by its neighborhood, city, and state, but most importantly by its employees and customers. Both are likely to be owners, as the brewery is a true cooperative with more than 1,500 current members. Fair State is proof that beer not only can bring people together but also do good.

Heat a large cast-iron or nonstick pan over high heat. Add the chicken livers and sear, turning, for about 2 minutes on each side, or until browned. Transfer the chicken livers to a plate and set aside. Add the shallots and garlic to the skillet and cook, stirring frequently, for 1 minute, or until fragrant.

Transfer the shallots and garlic to a food processor or blender. Add the chicken livers, cognac, brown sugar, oregano, and thyme. Add the cream mixture then blend until incorporated into a paste. With the food processor running, slowly add the remaining 1 cup (2 sticks) of butter, 1 Tbsp at a time, and blend until fully incorporated.

Transfer to a serving bowl, cover, and refrigerate for 30 minutes before serving. When ready serve with crackers.

SPRING GREENS SALAD WITH LEMON IPA VINAIGRETTE AND GRILLED TROUT

Serves 4

VINAIGRETTE
2 garlic cloves, minced
1 small shallot, minced
½ cup honey
½ cup fresh lemon juice
¼ cup hazy IPA, such as
    Sierra Nevada Hazy Little
    Thing IPA
¼ cup whole grain mustard
½ tsp kosher salt
1 cup blended oil (combining
    canola oil and olive oil)

SALAD
12 oz mixed spring greens
1 cup blueberries
2 peaches, halved and
    thinly sliced
4 oz blue cheese, crumbled
1 cup toasted pecans

TROUT
¼ cup extra-virgin olive oil
2 Tbsp canola oil
Four 6 oz skinless trout fillets
Kosher salt and freshly ground
    black pepper

Sierra Nevada Brewing Co.
MILLS RIVER, NORTH CAROLINA

The Pairing: Bavarian-Style Wheat Beer

Salads can be dressed up with protein in any number of ways, but adding freshly grilled trout brings delicious nutty flavor to the plate. In this recipe from the Sierra Nevada taproom, it combines beautifully with the sweetness of blueberries, the tang of blue cheese, and the crunch of pecans. Although the vinaigrette calls for a hazy IPA as an ingredient, the ideal beverage pairing is a Bavarian-style wheat, which just sings with the lemon in the vinaigrette. Sierra Nevada makes one such beer, named Kellerweis, which is served at their pubs. This recipe makes about two cups of dressing, which can be stored in an airtight container in the refrigerator for up to one week.

To make the vinaigrette: In a blender or food processor, combine the garlic, shallot, honey, lemon juice, beer, mustard, and salt and purée until well combined. With the blender or food processor on, gradually add the blended oil and continue to process until fully incorporated, being careful not to break the vinaigrette.

To make the salad: In a medium bowl, combine the spring greens, blueberries, and peaches, and toss to combine. Drizzle with enough vinaigrette to lightly coat the greens and toss again. Transfer the salad to a plate, piling it into a tall mound. Top with the blue cheese and pecans and set aside while you grill the fish.

To make the trout: Heat a grill or grill pan over high heat. Combine the olive oil and canola oil and rub all over each trout fillet to completely coat. Season with salt and pepper. Place the trout directly on the grill grates or in the grill pan and grill for 3 minutes, or until it starts to brown. Rotate the fillets slightly to create a diamond grill mark pattern and grill for 3 more minutes. Flip the fillets over and grill for 3 to 5 minutes, or until cooked through. Remove from the grill, arrange on top of the salad, and serve.

Sierra Nevada Brewing Co.

One of the oldest craft breweries in America, Sierra Nevada is also likely the most influential. With the 1980 release of its flagship pale ale, it attuned generations of palates to the pleasure of hops. Continually innovating as a source for sustainability initiatives, agricultural advancement, and recipe development, this company has two locations, the first in Chico, California, and a newer brewery in Mills River, North Carolina, which is known as "Malt Disney World."

LEMONY WHITE BEAN AND SAUSAGE SOUP

Serves 6 to 8

- 1 bunch kale, or spinach, or arugula (or a combination of greens)
- 3 Tbsp extra-virgin olive oil, preferably infused with gremolata, plus additional for serving
- 1 large onion, diced
- 1 large carrot, diced
- 1 red, yellow, or orange bell pepper, diced
- 1 cup sliced mushrooms
- 1 Tbsp tomato paste
- 1 tsp ground cumin
- ⅛ tsp red pepper flakes, plus additional for serving
- 8 oz smoked sausage, cut into thin slices
- 3 garlic cloves, minced
- 1 Tbsp freshly grated ginger
- 4 cups vegetable stock
- Two 15 oz cans cannellini beans, drained and rinsed
- Juice of ½ lemon

Gotahold Brewing

EUREKA SPRINGS, ARKANSAS

The Pairing: Grisette

Wendy Reese Hartmann, co-owner of Gotahold Brewing, calls this "Summer Dreamin' Soup," because its bright freshness conjures dreams of warm days to come, even in the dead of winter. Hartmann's recipe involves slow cooking on the stove, but this soup can also be made in a multicooker like an Instant Pot for fewer dishes in the sink. If you have olive oil infused with gremolata—the Italian herbal combination of lemon zest, garlic, and parsley—Reese Hartmann suggests using that. Otherwise, a high-quality extra-virgin olive oil will do. Pair the soup with grisette, a mild wheat farmhouse ale that has aromas and flavors reminiscent of a breezy country field. This should be served hot with bruschetta or sourdough bread slathered with garlic butter.

Pull the kale leaves off the stems and discard the stems. Tear or chop the leaves into bite-size pieces, place in an airtight container, and refrigerate until ready to use.

In a Dutch oven or other heavy pot, heat the olive oil over medium heat for about 30 seconds, or until shimmering. Add the onion, carrot, bell pepper, and mushrooms and cook, stirring occasionally, for 3 to 5 minutes, or until the onion is translucent. Add tomato paste, cumin, and red pepper flakes. Stir to combine, and sauté 1 minute. Add the sausage, garlic, ginger, stock, and beans, stir to combine, and cover. Turn the heat to low and simmer, adding more stock as needed, for 2 to 3 hours, or until ready to serve.

If using an Instant Pot, use the sauté function and add the oil and heat until it shimmers, about 30 seconds, then add the onion, carrot, bell pepper, and mushrooms and cook, stirring occasionally, for 3 to 5 minutes. Stir in tomato paste, cumin, and red pepper flakes. Turn off the sauté function then add the sausage, garlic, ginger, stock, and beans. Set the Instant Pot to the slow cooker function and cook for 10 to 12 hours, or until ready to serve.

About 10 minutes before serving, add the chilled greens and the lemon juice to the soup, stir, and cover to keep warm.

Drizzle with olive oil and sprinkle with more red-pepper flakes, if desired.

Gotahold Brewing

After a career spent at the helm of prestigious New England breweries, Dave Hartmann moved south and opened Gotahold with his wife, Wendy. There, in their modest taproom, Dave makes beers that inspire conversation and foster it as well. In an area of the country that had previously been lacking a small brewery, the couple is educating the local beer curious about the brewing process and promoting ales and lagers while also building a community.

SHROOMIN' PHILLY WITH AGAVE MUSTARD

Serves 2

½ cup stone ground mustard

¼ cup organic agave syrup

2 Tbsp vegan mayonnaise (soy free if necessary)

1 lb oyster or portobello mushrooms, trimmed and cut into ¼ in slices

2 bell peppers, cut into ¼ in slices

1 medium sweet Vidalia onion, cut into ¼ in slices

1 Tbsp garlic powder

4 slices vegan provolone, such as Violife

2 hoagie rolls, toasted if desired

Lost Worlds Brewing

CORNELIUS, NORTH CAROLINA

The Pairing: American Wheat

Chef Sasha Quinn of the Soul Miner's Garden food truck created this vegan take on the beloved Philadelphia cheese steak sandwich. It can easily be scaled up for crowds. Pair it with an American wheat beer, one that has a little bit of herbal spice and breadiness that will go a long way to boost both the veggies and the sweet and spicy mustard.

In a small bowl, whisk together the mustard, agave syrup, and mayonnaise until well combined.

In a large skillet, cook the mushrooms, bell peppers, and onions over medium heat, stirring frequently, for 5 to 10 minutes, or until the mushrooms have released their liquid and the onions have started to brown. Season with garlic powder. Divide the mixture in the skillet into two sections and top each with two slices of cheese. Cook for 2 minutes, or until the cheese is melted. Spread some of the agave mustard on the inside of each hoagie roll. Transfer the veggie and cheese mixture to the rolls and serve.

Lost Worlds Brewing
While relatively new as a brewery, Lost Worlds has an experienced brewing team turning out beers that capture an adventurous spirit. From lagers and dark ales that are rooted in tradition but sometimes reveal modern twists, the beers are flavorful and inviting, the kind of pints that foster conversation between friends, old and new alike.

CROQUE MADAME WITH BEER PRETZEL BREAD

Serves 4

BREAD

¼ cup dunkelweizen
¼ cup light brown sugar
2 tsp fine sea salt, plus additional for sprinkling
2½ tsp instant yeast
2½ cups all-purpose flour, plus additional for dusting
3 Tbsp unsalted butter, at room temperature
⅓ cup baking soda
1 large egg, beaten

BÉCHAMEL

3 cups whole milk, warm
1 cup heavy cream, warm
5 Tbsp unsalted butter, at room temperature
3 Tbsp all-purpose flour
1 tsp ground nutmeg
¼ tsp chili powder
2 oz shredded sharp Cheddar cheese
2 oz shredded Swiss cheese, plus 8 slices Swiss cheese
2 oz shredded Asiago
2 large egg yolks

continues ↗

Pacifica Brewery

PACIFICA, CALIFORNIA

The Pairing: Dunkelweizen

A decadent sandwich that combines salty and savory fillings with freshly baked rolls adds some pizzazz to lunchtime. Putting dunkelweizen in the dough and in the glass adds a roasted, sweet, and slightly spicy element that complements both the creaminess of the cheese and the saltiness of the ham. Serve with a sunny-side up egg on top (optional) and a mixed green salad or French fries.

To make the bread: In the bowl of a stand mixer, whisk together 1½ cups of lukewarm water, beer, brown sugar, and salt. Sprinkle the yeast on top and combine. Add the flour and butter and transfer the bowl to the stand mixer. Using the dough hook, knead the mixture for about 5 minutes, or until smooth.

Cover the bowl with plastic wrap and let proof at room temperature for about 30 minutes, or until doubled in size.

Preheat the oven to 400°F. Line a baking sheet with parchment paper.

Fill a large pot with water, add the baking soda, and bring to a boil.

Transfer the proofed dough to a floured surface, divide into 8 equal portions, and shape into oval loaves. Set the loaves on the prepared baking sheet and let proof in a warm area for 10 minutes.

Working in batches, carefully lower the proofed loaves into the boiling water, turning once, for 40 seconds. Remove from the water and return to the baking sheet.

Whisk the egg with 1 Tbsp of water to make an egg wash and brush on the tops of the loaves. Use a sharp knife to score the tops of the loaves then sprinkle with salt. Bake for 30 minutes, or until golden brown and cooked through. Allow to rest.

Pacifica Brewery

A number of breweries that have opened in the last few years focus solely on the taproom experience, but Pacifica hearkens back to the brewpub days and runs a gastropub where pairings are the focus. With a brewery helmed by Kim Sturdavant, a longtime Bay Area brewer, Pacifica's beers impressed right out of the gate and a new local favorite was born.

Fine sea salt and freshly
   ground black pepper
4 slices French or other high-
   quality ham
—
1 Tbsp olive oil (optional)
4 large eggs (optional)

To make the béchamel: In a medium bowl, whisk together the warm milk and cream.

In a medium saucepan, melt 3 Tbsp of the butter over medium heat. Add the flour and cook, whisking constantly, for about 3 minutes, or until golden brown. Add the nutmeg and chili powder and whisk to combine. Slowly add the milk mixture and whisk to combine. Turn the heat to low and cook for about 10 minutes, or until the sauce thickens. Gradually add the shredded cheeses, whisking constantly until melted. Remove from the heat, add the egg yolks, and whisk until fully incorporated. Season with salt and pepper. Keep warm.

To make the sandwiches: Preheat the oven to 200°F.

Slice the loaves, spread the remaining 2 Tbsp of butter on the cut sides, and arrange on a baking sheet. Put a slice of Swiss cheese on each bottom loaf and top with a slice of ham then another slice of Swiss cheese. Close the sandwiches and bake for about 10 minutes, or until warmed through. If serving each sandwich with an egg on top, add the olive oil to a large saute pan or skillet on medium heat, and fry the eggs until desired yolk consistency. Arrange the sandwiches on plates and top with the béchamel and fried egg (if using).

TEMPURA-BATTERED SHRIMP TACOS

Serves 4 to 6

SALSA

1 large pineapple, peeled, cored, and diced

2 mangoes, halved, pitted, peeled, and dice

2 red bell peppers, diced

2 small jalapeños, diced

8 scallions, sliced

1 cup chopped fresh cilantro

3 Tbsp dark brown sugar, plus additional as needed

Juice of 3 limes, plus additional fresh lime juice as needed

1 Tbsp tamari

1½ tsp extra-virgin olive oil

1 tsp sesame oil

Fine sea salt and freshly ground black pepper

SHRIMP

¾ cup cornstarch

¼ cup rice flour or all-purpose flour

½ tsp baking powder

½ tsp smoked paprika

½ tsp dark chili powder

⅛ tsp cayenne pepper

1 large egg, lightly beaten

½ cup seltzer or sparkling water

Vegetable oil, for frying

1 lb shrimp, peeled, deveined, and tail removed

8 flour or corn tortillas

Sour cream, for serving (optional)

Wallenpaupack Brewing Co.

HAWLEY, PENNSYLVANIA

The Pairing: Hefeweizen

This is one of the most popular dishes at this Pocono Mountains area brewpub. Maybe it's because the flavors evoke warm weather and have a light, easy bite that fuels you for the fun summer activities ahead. Making shrimp tacos at home and pairing them with a hefeweizen—one with light banana and clove undertones—brings brighter days right to your dining room table.

To make the salsa: In a large bowl combine the pineapple, mangoes, bell peppers, jalapeños, scallions, cilantro, brown sugar, lime juice, tamari, olive oil, and sesame oil. Toss to combine then season with salt and pepper. Taste the salad and add more lime juice if it's too sweet or more brown sugar if it's too tart. Refrigerate until ready to use.

To make the shrimp: In a large bowl, whisk together the cornstarch, rice flour, baking powder, paprika, chili powder, and cayenne pepper. Add the egg and seltzer and mix until a smooth batter forms.

Fill a wok, deep pot, or deep fryer with about 1 in of vegetable oil and heat to 350°F on a thermometer. Line a plate with paper towels. Working in batches, dip the shrimp in the batter, shaking off any excess, then carefully add to the oil and fry, turning occasionally, for about 2 minutes, or until golden brown. Transfer the shrimp to the paper towel–lined plate to drain. Fry the remaining shrimp, adjusting the heat as needed to keep the oil at 350°F.

In a medium cast-iron or nonstick pan, warm the tortillas over medium heat for about 30 seconds per side. Transfer the hot tortillas to plates and top with shrimp and then salsa. Serve with sour cream (if using).

Wallenpaupack Brewing Co.

In the middle of the year-round outdoorsy joyland that is the Pocono Mountains of Pennsylvania, Wallenpaupack Brewing Co. opened several years ago with a commitment to bring fresh, high-quality, locally made beer to vacationers and residents alike. With approachable lagers, inventive IPAs, and a desire to educate through obscure styles, this brewery has grown quickly, as new fans find their way into their expansive and impressive tasting room.

Sour Ales

While the word *sour* might conjure up unpleasant thoughts, sour ales are darlings among craft beer lovers. It's smarter and more accurate, however, to use the word *tart* to describe these beers.

Despite their classifications, sours are actually a great way to get wine lovers to explore beer. They can have a pronounced fruity, tangy, or spicy character from the *Lactobacillus* probiotic, or a citrus-like acidity. Some come with Champagne-like carbonation. But overall, the complexity of the style, when done well, is a marvel in the glass.

The main beers you are likely to encounter in the wild are Berliner Weisse and Gose, although there's also the darker and more savory Flanders red ale and Oud Bruin, as well as the relatively new Sour IPA.

While it can be hard to find an unflavored Berliner Weisse or Gose, they are worth seeking out. They can have a salty or savory kick, and as they usually are low in alcohol, these refreshing beers are built to be sessionable, suitable for multiple rounds at the bar. Both are popular with athletes after workouts and races.

There aren't too many sours on the market that are traditional versions of the style. More often, brewers use sour ales as a canvas to highlight adjunct ingredients, usually fruit. From pineapple and mango to passion fruit, dragon fruit, and hibiscus, these salty, sweet, and sometimes acidic combinations make sour ales a delight with food.

While the delicateness of the style lends itself to lighter foods, focusing on some of the more assertive flavors can make for great food pairings. Think dandelion salad or grilled chicken with olives, or even use the beer itself as an ingredient in a vinaigrette. Sours are also ideal brunch beers that stand up nicely to avocado toast, whole-wheat pancakes, and parfaits.

DORITO-CRUSTED SCOTCH EGGS WITH CUMIN-FENNEL MARMALADE AND PICKLED FENNEL FRONDS

Serves 2

PICKLED FENNEL FRONDS
½ cup white wine vinegar
¼ cup homemade or store-
    bought pickling spice
20 fennel fronds

SCOTCH EGGS
4 large eggs
4 cups grapeseed oil
2 Tbsp oat milk
1 cup all-purpose flour
1 cup panko breadcrumbs
1 cup finely crushed Doritos
6 oz ground chicken
Zest of 1 orange
1 Tbsp chopped fresh oregano
1 tsp crushed juniper berries
Fine sea salt and freshly
    ground black pepper

continues ↗

New Realm Brewing Co.

ATLANTA, GEORGIA

The Pairing: Gose

Scotch eggs are a brewery staple. Hearty and indulgent, they're ideal for brunch, especially when the night before was a little wild. This version plays into excess and offers a modern, junk food–accented twist. A Gose, with its low abv, slightly salty notes, and generally refreshing nature, is a great pairing. It won't weigh down your palate and leans into the richer parts of the dish. Note: If pickling your own fennel fronds, allow for a day of preparation. And if you're grinding the chicken at home, opt for half breast meat and half dark meat.

To make the pickled fennel fronds: In a large jar or other airtight container, combine the white wine vinegar, pickling spice, and fennel fronds. Add ½ cup of water, shake to combine, and refrigerate for between 2 and 24 hours.

To make the eggs: Bring a small pot of water to boil over high heat. Fill a bowl with ice water.

Add 2 of the eggs to the boiling water and cook for 8 minutes then transfer to the ice water and let rest for 1 minute. Carefully peel the shells from the eggs and pat the eggs dry with a paper towel.

Fill a large Dutch oven, deep pot, or deep fryer with 1 in of the grapeseed oil and heat to 325°F on a thermometer. Line a plate with paper towels.

Break the remaining 2 eggs into a shallow bowl with oat milk and lightly beat. Put the flour, panko breadcrumbs, and Doritos in separate shallow bowls.

In a large bowl, combine the ground chicken, orange zest, oregano, and juniper berries. Season with salt and pepper. Form half of the chicken mixture into a thin patty and then wrap the patty around 1 of the cooked eggs. Dip the chicken-wrapped egg in the flour, followed by the eggs, the panko breadcrumbs, and the Doritos. Repeat with the remaining cooked egg.

Carefully add the eggs to the oil and fry, turning occasionally, for 3 to 5 minutes, or until golden brown. Transfer to the paper towel–lined plate.

CUMIN-FENNEL MARMALADE

1 large fennel bulb, trimmed and chopped

¼ cup hazelnut oil

1 Tbsp cumin seeds, toasted and crushed

Fine sea salt and freshly ground black pepper

Extra-virgin olive oil, for drizzling

To make the cumin-fennel marmalade: Bring a large pot of water to a boil over high heat. Add the chopped fennel and cook for about 20 minutes, or until tender. Drain the fennel and transfer to a food processor or blender. Add the hazelnut oil and cumin seeds, season with salt and pepper, and blend until the mixture forms a purée.

Cut the Scotch eggs lengthwise in half and arrange on a serving plate. Spoon some cumin-fennel marmalade on the plate, drizzle with olive oil, and top with the pickled fennel fronds. Finish with black pepper and serve immediately.

New Realm Brewing Co.

In the few short years that it has been open, this brewery, helmed by some industry veteran heavyweights, has not only delivered on an outstanding beer and food program but has grown its footprint as well. Now with locations in Virginia and an outpost in Savannah (that also includes a distillery), New Realm is making lagers and ales that enhance the drinking experience.

SPICY SHRIMP COCKTAIL

Serves 4 to 6

1 lb cooked medium shrimp
1 cup tomato juice
½ cup ketchup
¼ cup fresh lime juice
2 Tbsp hot sauce, such as
  Tapatío or Valentina
¼ cup minced fresh cilantro
1 tsp fine sea salt
½ tsp freshly ground black
  pepper
2 Roma tomatoes, diced with
  juices reserved
1 cucumber, seeded and diced
½ cup diced red onion
1 jalapeño, seeded and diced
1 avocado, sliced
Saltine crackers, for serving

Cosmic Eye Brewing

LINCOLN, NEBRASKA

The Pairing: American Sour

You might wonder what a Nebraska brewery knows about shrimp, but it turns out that the state's farmers have turned to aquaculture over the years and are now producing sustainable seafood. This dish from Chef Michael Vandenberg pairs well with a quick American kettle sour. The lactic acid in the beer plays up the citrus acidity and saltiness of the dish.

Chop half of the shrimp into small pieces and leave the rest whole. Set aside.

In a large bowl, whisk together the tomato juice, ketchup, lime juice, hot sauce, cilantro, salt, and pepper. Add the tomatoes and their juices, and the cucumber, red onion, and jalapeño and fold to fully combine. Gently fold in the chopped shrimp. Transfer to a serving dish and arrange the avocado slices and whole shrimp on top in an attractive design. Cover and chill for at least 1 hour. Serve chilled with saltine crackers.

Cosmic Eye Brewing
Beer doesn't need to be fussy, but it should provoke thought. At Cosmic Eye, the brewing team, led by Sam Riggins, works to create well-executed "deceptively simple traditional beers" designed for easy drinking. From lagers to pale ales, the brewery is making beers suited for nights out, tailgating, and cookouts in the yard with family.

AIR-FRIED CHICKEN WINGS WITH HONEY BARBECUE SAUCE

Serves 2 to 4

HONEY BARBECUE SAUCE

1 Tbsp unsalted butter
1 large yellow onion, thinly
    sliced
1 cup barbecue sauce
¼ cup mayonnaise
2 Tbsp molasses
2 Tbsp honey, plus additional
    for serving
½ tsp chopped fresh
    rosemary, OK to substitute
    dried
¼ tsp cayenne pepper
1 Tbsp fine sea salt
Coarse sea salt, for serving

WINGS

2 dozen fresh chicken drums
    and flats
Fine sea salt

Stone Cow Brewery

BARRE, MASSACHUSETTS

The Pairing: Kettle Sour Ale

Air frying wings is a quick and easy way to make this full-flavored chicken snack without the need for oil. It comes together quickly, and the sauce, created by brewery co-owner Molly Stevens DuBois, is great on other dishes as well. In addition to the dipping sauce, you can serve these wings with more honey and a sprinkle of coarse sea salt. A low-abv, slightly tart and low acid sour ale, especially one flavored with hibiscus, is an ideal pairing.

To make the sauce: In a small frying pan, melt the butter over medium heat. Add the onion and cook, stirring occasionally, for about 20 minutes, or until well caramelized. Transfer the onions to a food processor then add the barbecue sauce, mayonnaise, molasses, honey, rosemary, cayenne pepper, and salt. Blend until fully combined and smooth. Transfer half the sauce to a large bowl; reserve the rest for dipping.

To make the wings: Pat the chicken drums and flats dry with paper towels, sprinkle with salt, and let stand for 15 minutes then pat dry again. Arrange the wings in a single layer in the fryer basket of an air fryer. Cook at 365°F for 12 minutes. Flip the wings and cook for 5 more minutes, until golden with some char.

Transfer the wings to the bowl of sauce and toss to coat. Increase the air fryer temperature to 380°F then return the wings to the basket and cook for 5 more minutes, or until the sauce has caramelized. Serve immediately with the reserved sauce for dipping—and a lot of napkins.

Stone Cow Brewery

There are few spots as idyllic to drink a beer than the expansive farm that is home to Stone Cow Brewery. It's an actual working dairy farm, and much of the food that is served from the on-site kitchen is locally sourced. For five generations, the Stevens family has been working the land, bringing fresh natural items to patrons. Their beer is the latest venture that helps bring great experiences to the land.

MUSHROOM PASTA

Serves 4

1 lb mushrooms, preferably wild chanterelles or porcinis, or store-bought varieties such as cremini, oyster, or shiitake

1 lb fettuccini

¼ cup olive oil

2 Tbsp unsalted butter

4 garlic cloves, finely chopped

2 medium shallots or 1 small yellow onion, finely chopped

Fine sea salt and freshly ground black pepper

¼ cup mixed-culture golden sour beer

½ cup heavy cream

Juice of 1 lemon

Freshly grated Parmesan cheese, for serving

Fresh flat-leaf parsley, for serving

The Starkeller

NEW ULM, MINNESOTA

The Pairing: Barrel-Aged Mixed-Culture Farmhouse Ale

This is a great recipe when made with freshly picked wild mushrooms but can be made with store-bought varieties as well. Former Starkeller brewer Jace Marti created this recipe and says the sour beer reduction adds flavor to the mushrooms and helps create a creamy, decadent sauce. This is a rich, luxurious recipe but can be made quite quickly and can be enjoyed any night of the week.

Cut or break the mushrooms into quarters or thick slices, depending on the type of mushrooms you are using. Set aside.

Bring a large pot of salted water to a boil. Add the pasta and cook, according to the packaging instructions, 1 to 2 minutes short of al dente. Drain the pasta, reserving at least ¼ cup of the pasta cooking water.

Meanwhile, in a large skillet, heat the olive oil over medium-high heat until shimmering. Add the mushrooms, stir to coat in the oil, and then allow to sear, undisturbed, for about 5 minutes, or until starting to turn golden brown. Stir and then sear again for about 7 to 10 minutes, or until evenly browned. Add the butter, garlic, and shallots and cook, stirring frequently, for 1 to 2 minutes, or until the garlic and shallots are golden and fragrant and the mushrooms have sweat out. Season with salt and pepper. Add the beer, turn the heat to medium, and simmer for about 5 minutes or until the beer is slightly reduced. Add the heavy cream and simmer for about 2 more minutes, or until the liquid is reduced by a quarter. Add the lemon juice, taste the sauce, and season as needed with salt and pepper.

Add the cooked pasta to the mushroom mixture, along with the reserved pasta cooking water. Cook, stirring to coat the pasta in sauce, for about 4 minutes, or until the pasta water is absorbed and the sauce has thickened slightly. Remove from the heat and allow the pasta to stand for a few minutes—the sauce will continue to thicken as it cools.

Sprinkle with Parmesan cheese and parsley and serve.

The Starkeller

Beer has always been the family business at the August Schell Brewing Co., but rather than follow the status quo, Jace Marti, a sixth-generation family brewer, worked to bring the brewery into new arenas, notably by making wild and wood-aged beers through the Starkeller Brewery Noble Star collection. Thanks to some long-forgotten equipment, namely foeders, or large wooden fermentation vessels, that were refurbished and moved to a separate location in town, the brewery that has long been known for bocks and lagers is now gaining acclaim for vibrant ales with fruit additions and great depth.

GRILLED NORTH CAROLINA GROUPER WITH PISTACHIO ROMESCO, SUGAR SNAP PEAS, AND SALSA VERDE

Serves 4

ROMESCO

⅓ cup roasted, salted pistachios

6 oz fresh hot Hatch (or New Mexican red) chiles (OK to substitute jarred and strained)

1 garlic clove

2 Tbsp chopped fresh flat-leaf parsley

2 Tbsp sherry vinegar

Fine sea salt and freshly ground black pepper

⅓ cup spinach

6 tablespoons extra-virgin olive oil

continues ↗

Resident Culture Brewing Co.

CHARLOTTE, NORTH CAROLINA

The Pairing: Sour Ale

This recipe comes from Kindred restaurant in Davidson, North Carolina. The grilled grouper makes a bright, clean, green accompaniment to a sour ale like Resident Culture Brewery's Vibe Check, a sour ale made with local peaches. Grouper, a fish known to North Carolina waters, also adds a layer of local flavor to the finished pairing. Don't let the hot hatch chiles or chili flakes worry you—it all balances out to a mild, flavorful, herbaceous, and citrusy dish that complements a sour ale's aromatic nose and lively acidity.

To make the romesco: In a food processor, combine the pistachios, Hatch chiles, garlic, and parsley and pulse until a loose paste forms. Add the vinegar, ½ tsp of salt, and ¼ tsp of pepper and pulse to combine. Add the spinach then turn on the food processor and very slowly drizzle in the olive oil, blending until the romesco has the consistency of peanut butter—it should be bright green. Set aside. (The romesco can be refrigerated in an airtight container for about 1 week.)

To make the salsa verde: In a bowl, combine the shallot, Meyer lemon juice, and ¾ tsp salt. Stir to combine. Add the olive oil, parsley, cilantro, chili flakes (if using), and the Meyer lemon zest. Season with salt and pepper and toss to combine. Set aside. (The salsa can be refrigerated in an airtight container for about 1 week.)

To make the grouper: Heat a gas or charcoal grill to high and coat the grill grates with cooking spray.

Thoroughly pat the grouper fillets dry with paper towels and season with salt and pepper.

> *Resident Culture Brewing Co.*
> *This brewery is not only a great place to absorb the local neighborhood vibe but, thanks to its coolship, a fermentation vessel that is exposed to the elements, it's possible to taste the neighborhood as well. Resident Culture Brewing has cultivated a wild ale program that plays off the best of North Carolina, but what you'll also experience is a company culture that thrives on community and collaboration, adding an extra layer of satisfaction to each pint.*

SALSA VERDE

1 small shallot, minced

Zest and juice of 1 Meyer lemon

Fine sea salt and freshly ground black pepper

¼ cup extra-virgin olive oil

1 Tbsp finely chopped fresh flat-leaf parsley

1 Tbsp finely chopped fresh cilantro

¼ tsp chili flakes (optional)

GROUPER

Four 6 oz grouper fillets, skin on

SUGAR SNAP PEAS

1 Tbsp olive oil

8 oz sugar snap peas

1 Tbsp unsalted butter

Zest and juice of 1 Meyer lemon

Fine sea salt

Put the grouper, skin-side down, directly on the grates and grill for 4 minutes then flip and grill for 2 more minutes, or until the thickest part of the fish reaches 145°F on a thermometer. Let the grouper rest while you make the sugar snap peas.

To make the sugar snap peas: In a medium saucepan, heat the olive oil over high heat until shimmering. Add the sugar snap peas and cook, tossing frequently, for 2 minutes. Add the butter and cook, tossing frequently, until the butter is melted and has glazed the peas. Remove from the heat, add the Meyer lemon zest and juice, and season with salt. Keep warm.

Divide the romesco evenly between 4 plates, spreading it to cover the plate. Spoon the snap peas over the romesco and top with the grouper. Drizzle the salsa verde over the grouper and serve immediately.

PAN-SEARED HALIBUT WITH GOSE BUTTER SAUCE AND ROASTED VEGETABLES

Crane Brewing Co.

RAYTOWN, MISSOURI

The Pairing: Fruited Gose

Fruit and fish are wonderful complements when done right. This is one such example, courtesy of Chef Chad Tillman of Crane Brewing, who suggests using a fruited Gose in the sauce. Specifically, the Crane Brewing Gooseberry, but other flavors available in your market will also work. "Missouri doesn't have citrus that grows well here so we have to adapt. Gooseberries are a great substitute when looking for some tartness in a dish," says Tillman. This can be a quick weeknight meal or one for impressing dinner guests that comes together fast. Serve the same beer you used in the sauce and enjoy.

Serves 2

- 1 baby bok choy, halved lengthwise
- 1 lb rainbow carrots, peeled and cut into ¼ in thick coins
- Fine sea salt and freshly ground black pepper
- 1 tsp vegetable oil
- Two 6 oz halibut fillets, skin removed
- ¼ cup fruited Gose
- ½ shallot, minced
- 2 Tbsp honey
- 2 Tbsp unsalted butter

Preheat the oven to 400°F. Lightly oil a baking sheet. Put the bok choy, cut-side up, and carrots on the baking sheet and season with salt and pepper. Roast for 20 minutes, or until the vegetables start to soften and lightly brown. Keep warm.

Meanwhile, in a nonstick pan, heat the vegetable oil over medium heat until shimmering. Season both sides of the halibut fillets with salt and pepper and put in the pan. Cook, flipping once, for 3 to 5 minutes per side, or until the internal temperature reaches 145°F on a thermometer. Transfer to plate to rest. Add the beer and deglaze the pan, using a wooden spoon to scrape any browned bits off the bottom. Add the shallot and honey and cook, stirring frequently, for 3 to 5 minutes, or until thickened. Add the butter and stir to melt and incorporate.

Divide the vegetables between 2 plates and place the halibut on top. Drizzle with the glaze and serve immediately.

> ### Crane Brewing Co.
> Talk to Chris Meyers, cofounder of Crane Brewing Co., and he'll describe the brewery as inspired equally by the bold craft beers of America and the rustic ales of Europe. The brewers aspire to make dry and rustic ales like those of Wallonia and the Senne Valley in Belgium and are harvesting yeast and propagating it in their in-house laboratory. Meyers says they take traditional methods seriously but also have a few ideas of their own. They call it "tradition, evolving."

SMOKED ADOBO CHICKEN

Serves 4

½ cup plus 1 Tbsp kosher salt
¼ cup granulated sugar
4 boneless chicken breasts
2 Tbsp vegetable oil
Juice of 1 orange
Juice of 1 lime
4½ Tbsp soy sauce
3 tsp achiote (annatto)
   powder
6 chiles de árbol
1 dried ancho chile
2 garlic cloves
½ tsp ground cumin
Ensalada de Casa with
   Cilantro-Lime Vinaigrette
   and Peach Pico de Gallo
   (recipe follows)

Von Ebert Brewing

PORTLAND, OREGON

The Pairing: Fruited Farmhouse Ale

Adobo chicken, a favorite at the brewery, can be smoked or baked and pairs well with a wood or foeder-aged farmhouse ale. The brewery's Alma is fermented with *Brettanomyces* yeast and locally grown organic peaches. Or look for fruited mixed-culture beers with balanced or low acidity that are fermented with fruit that pairs with the Peach Pico de Gallo (following recipe). Like raspberry, blueberry, cherry, or red currants. Achieving the full flavor of this dish requires brining and marinating, so be sure to plan ahead.

In a large bowl, combine ½ cup of the salt with the sugar and 8 cups of water and stir to combine.

Place the chicken, curved-side up, on a cutting board. Use a knife to split the chicken down the center of the breast and spread open. Put in a container large enough to hold the chicken and brine. Cover the chicken with the brine and refrigerate overnight or for up to 24 hours.

In a blender, combine the vegetable oil, orange juice, lime juice, soy sauce, achiote powder, chiles de árbol, ancho chile, garlic, cumin, and the remaining 1 Tbsp of salt. Blend until fully combined into a paste.

Remove the chicken from the brine and pat dry with paper towels. Rub the chile paste evenly all over the chicken. (Leftover paste can be frozen in an airtight container for up to 1 month.) Cover and refrigerate for 2 hours.

If using a smoker, smoke for 1 hour and 15 minutes or until the internal temperature reaches 165°F. Alternatively, preheat the oven to 350°F. Put the chicken in a roasting pan or on a baking sheet and bake for 45 minutes, or until the internal temperature reaches 165°F on a thermometer. Serve with the Ensalada de Casa with Cilantro-Lime Vinaigrette and Peach Pico de Gallo.

ENSALADA DE CASA WITH CILANTRO LIME VINAIGRETTE AND PEACH PICO DE GALLO

Serves 4

PICO DE GALLO
1 peach, cut into small dice
1 tomato, cut into small dice
½ medium yellow onion,
    cut into small dice
1 jalapeño or serrano pepper,
    seeded and minced
2 Tbsp minced fresh cilantro
1 Tbsp fresh lime juice
Fine sea salt

SALAD
2 cups salad greens
½ avocado, thinly sliced
¼ cup Cotija
¼ cup toasted pumpkin seeds
3 Tbsp pickled red onions

VINAIGRETTE
1 bunch fresh cilantro leaves
1 bunch scallions
3 jalapeños, stemmed and seeded
3 garlic cloves, minced
1½ cups fresh lime juice
    (from 12 limes)
3 cups canola oil
Fine sea salt

The Pairing: Fruited Farmhouse Ale

Von Ebert Brewing's house salad pairs exceptionally well with their Smoked Adobo Chicken (previous recipe), but it also works as a quick weekday lunch, while the salsa makes a great snack with chips.

To make the pico de gallo: In a medium bowl, combine the peach, tomato, onion, jalapeño, cilantro, and lime juice. Season with salt and toss to combine. Let stand, stirring occasionally, for 30 minutes at room temperature before serving.

To make the salad: In a large bowl, combine the salad greens, avocado, Cotija, pumpkin seeds, and pickled red onions. Toss to combine.

To make the vinaigrette: In a blender, combine the cilantro, scallions, jalapeños, garlic, and lime juice and blend until combined and smooth. With the blender on, gradually add the canola oil, blending until fully emulsified. Season with salt.

When ready to serve, toss the salad with about ¼ cup of the vinaigrette. (Leftover vinaigrette can be refrigerated in an airtight container for about a week.)

Von Ebert Brewing
A brewing company with several locations, Von Ebert Brewing is quickly making a name for itself in the Pacific Northwest. Owner Tom Cook and his team devote time and energy to exploring the relationship between farmhouse ales and wood along with locally grown fruits, as well as traditional styles that offer snappy hop-forward ales and crisp lagers.

Seasonal Beers

Beer moves with the seasons. While some styles are enjoyable year-round, others land differently in our minds and palates, depending on where we are on the calendar. Crisp lagers are "lawnmower" beers, thirst-quenching refreshments on hot summer afternoons, while bright and easy pale ales, with their delicate hop aroma and light, bready malt, speak to spring. Dark, strong ales like stouts and barleywines feel just right in winter, their higher abv warming us like a comfortable blanket. Wheat beers and saisons remind us of the harvest and changing seasons, and feel a little better in autumn.

Then there are the actual seasonal beers. In the same way that a farm stand offers different produce at different moments in the year, brewers often embrace the changing calendar with beers that fit the season or rely on the freshest ingredients being harvested.

Throughout the cold winter months, brewers tend to make a variety of strong ales and lagers. Chief among them are Eisbocks, strong beers that are brewed and then placed outside to freeze, which separates the water from the alcohol. The concentrated booze that's left behind is often filled with rich baked sugar and stone fruit flavors, and a small glass is almost better than any scarf or down jacket.

Bières de Nöel are strong Belgian ales, sometimes aged in barrels with spices and orange peel. When served at cellar temperature, they have attributes akin to a mulled beverage and are offered around Christmastime.

With spring come the Maibocks, which are stronger lagers that welcome in the warmer weather. Spring can also mean lighter beers that showcase honey or flowers.

Summer brings about shandies and radlers, beers mixed with fruit juice or other beverages to offer more refreshment and less alcohol. There are also summer ales and lagers, which are often citrus-accented, low-abv beers with moderate spice, designed to mimic sunshine in a glass.

Later in the summer, the wet-hopped and fresh-hopped beers begin to arrive. Brewed with just-picked-from-the-bine hop cones, which are added to fresh ale and lager recipes, they are bright and exciting, with a green vibrancy that is often missing in beers made with processed or dried hops the rest of the year.

Fresh-hopped beers typically fall into the IPA category since it is the style that benefits most from freshly picked hops, which bring a vivid aroma to an already hop-forward profile. They are usually brewed within twenty-four hours of the hops being picked, and often within mere hours. Brewers often work with farmers to get a few different hop varieties delivered and will make single-hopped beers to showcase the unique flavor and aroma profiles of each.

The majority of hops are grown in the Pacific Northwest, but other states, including New York, Michigan, Indiana, Illinois, and much of New England, grow them, too. With brewers in all these regions making fresh-hop beers, the chance to taste and pair food with this limited seasonal offering is now closer to home than ever before.

The closer a brewery is to a hop farm, the better, as the fresh hop season in the United States only runs from August to late September. Fresh-hop beers are often made in small quantities and served only at breweries, but there is a notable exception: Celebration is a fresh-hop IPA made and released each autumn through early winter by Sierra Nevada, the California brewery. Bright pine and citrus aromas burst forth from that beer, and because of its wide distribution, much of the country has the chance to experience its fresh flavors.

Autumn brings about specialty lagers and the famed Oktoberfest beer, which is made for drinking in large quantities. Traditional recipes call for this deep gold–colored lager to be in the high 4 percent abv range (with most American versions going higher). It should be slightly sweet, dry, bready, and malt-forward with little discernible hop character. It is, of course, synonymous with the festival of the same name, held each September in Munich.

Some breweries also use the season to release Märzen, lagers that were traditionally brewed in the spring (Märzen is German for March) and then lagered through the summer before being served in the fall. They are usually heavier than Oktoberfest beers, in the 6 percent abv range, and copper in color with a pronounced toasted malt character, little bitterness, and a dry finish.

We also have pumpkin beers, which should, more accurately, be called "pumpkin spice" beers, because cinnamon, nutmeg, allspice, and clove are the dominant flavors. From porters to lagers to amber ales, just about every style of beer has gotten the pumpkin treatment. While most appropriate to drink in autumn, many pumpkin beers show up on shelves as early as in July. Often these are made with canned rather than fresh pumpkin. For a true pumpkin beer experience, look for ones released in late October and throughout November that feature the real fruit.

As you drink seasonally, follow the lead from the markets. Find what is fresh and, as you think about dinner, give some thought to the beers that speak to the weather, the produce, and your mood. Finding a pint that jibes with the harvest calendar is always a smart move.

WAFFLES WITH BEER-BERRY COMPOTE

Serves 6 to 8

COMPOTE

1 cup mixed raspberries, blackberries, and blueberries
1 cup The Bog cranberry shandy or other berry shandy
¼ cup granulated sugar
1 tsp fresh lemon juice
1 strip fresh orange peel

WAFFLES

1 cup all-purpose flour
1 Tbsp granulated sugar
1 tsp baking powder
¼ tsp salt
1 cup whole milk
4 Tbsp (½ stick) unsalted butter, melted
2 large eggs
1 tsp pure vanilla extract

Cape May Brewing Co.

CAPE MAY, NEW JERSEY

The Pairing: Shandy

When the berries at the farmer's market are just too gorgeous to resist and you buy more than you need, this is the recipe to make. Add a few pantry staples and some fruit-forward beer, and soon breakfast is ready. The sweetness or tartness of the berries varies throughout the year, so feel free to increase or pull back on the sugar in the compote. Shandies are often lower in alcohol and big on fruity flavors, making it ideal for brunch-time imbibing. In the cooler months, try adding pinches of nutmeg and cinnamon to the berries for a festive variation.

To make the compote: In a medium saucepan combine the berries, beer, sugar, lemon juice, and orange peel and bring to boil over high heat. Continue boiling for 1 minute then turn the heat to medium-low and simmer vigorously for 7 minutes, or until the berries burst open, releasing their liquid. Continue simmering for 15 to 20 minutes, or until the liquid is reduced by half. Remove from the heat, discard orange peel, and allow to cool slightly before serving.

To make the waffles: In the bowl of a stand mixer fitted with the paddle attachment, whisk together the flour, sugar, baking powder, and salt until well combined. Add the milk, butter, eggs, and vanilla and beat until a batter forms. Alternatively, use a large bowl and a handheld mixer.

Preheat a waffle iron according to the manufacturer's instructions. Set a baking sheet in the oven and preheat the oven to 200°F to keep the waffles warm.

Add enough batter to the waffle iron to fully cover the surface and cook for 2 to 3 minutes, or until golden brown. Keep the waffles in the warm oven while you cook the rest of the batter. Serve immediately with the berry compote.

Cape May Brewing Co.
There is some delightful beer action happening at the southern tip of the Jersey Shore. From a facility inside an airport, this decade-old brewery has become a destination and source of Garden State pride, thanks to their flavored IPAs, shandies, seasonal offerings, and more.

GRILLED SHISHITO PEPPERS WITH LIME AND SALT

Serves 4 to 6

2 lbs shishito or Padrón
  peppers
1 Tbsp extra-virgin olive oil
1 Tbsp fresh lime juice
1 tsp fine sea salt

Bend Brewing Company

BEND, OREGON

The Pairing: Fresh Hop IPA

Zach Beckwith, the head brewer of Bend Brewing, is known for experimenting with and pushing the boundaries of fresh-hop beers, and when it comes to pairing them, he suggests building a charcuterie board. A few simple items, such as dill pickles (either homemade or from the farmer's market), high-quality aged salami, triple-cream Brie with a baguette, and an arugula salad will add to the hop experience. These grilled shishito peppers are super easy to make and are an excellent addition to the pairing experience. Shishitos are a mild pepper, although occasionally some have some heat, so eating them is always a bit of an adventure. The fat from the olive oil, the salt, and the flavorful pepper pair particularly nicely with fresh-hop beers.

Heat one side of a gas or charcoal grill to high; leave the other side cool.

In a large bowl, toss the peppers with the olive oil until well coated. Arrange the peppers on the cool side of the grill and cook over indirect heat for 4 to 6 minutes, or until they begin to wilt and char. Put the peppers in a serving bowl, toss with the lime juice and salt, and serve warm.

Bend Brewing Company
For nearly thirty years this brewpub has been an institution in a city and region known for great beer. With a rotating seasonal beer menu along with one-offs that strike a brewer's fancy, there is always something new on tap. The same is true with the food menu. While pub staples are offered, there are rotating specials that change with the seasons or offer fresh tastes on familiar dishes.

GRILLED PUMPKIN FLAT-BREAD WITH HOMEMADE RICOTTA AND HOT HONEY

Serves 4

FLATBREAD

2 Tbsp honey
2 tsp active dry yeast
3½ cups all-purpose flour
¼ cup pumpkin purée
1 large egg
2 garlic cloves, chopped
2 tsp kosher salt
½ tsp baking powder
2 Tbsp chopped fresh flat-leaf
    parsley

RICOTTA

4 cups whole milk
2 cups heavy cream
1 tsp kosher salt
3 Tbsp white wine vinegar
Freshly ground black pepper

HOT HONEY

¼ cup honey
2 tsp hot sauce

Two Roads Brewing Co.
STRATFORD, CONNECTICUT

The Pairing: Pumpkin Ale

What goes best with pumpkin beer? More pumpkin. Arguably one of the most popular seasonal beer styles, pumpkin beers are often about the baking spices that accompany the gourd, but the truly good ones have the earthy flavors of the autumnal fruit. Two Roads Brewing Co. makes one such ale, called Roadsmary's Baby, and this flatbread, the work of Chef Ryan Keelan, plays up the pumpkin flavor, while bringing in additional savory, sweet, and spicy elements for a snack that satisfies any time of year. You can make your own ricotta using this recipe or substitute a high-quality store-bought version.

To make the flatbread: In a medium bowl, stir together the honey and 1 cup of warm water until the honey has dissolved. Sprinkle in the yeast, stir, and let it stand for about 10 minutes, or until the yeast is foamy.

In a large bowl, combine the flour, pumpkin purée, egg, garlic, salt, and baking powder. Add the yeast mixture and mix with your hands until the dough is smooth but sticky and you're able to form it into a ball. Transfer the dough to a lightly floured surface and knead until soft.

Oil a large bowl, put the ball of dough inside, cover, and let rest for about 90 minutes, or until the dough has nearly doubled in size. Transfer the dough to a lightly floured surface and cut it into 8 equal pieces.

Heat a gas or charcoal grill to medium-high.

Roll each piece of dough into a thin circle. Put the flatbread rounds directly on grates and, working in batches, grill for 1 minute, or until bubbles form on the top. Flip the flatbreads and cook for 1 more minute, or until cooked through. Set aside and keep warm until ready to serve.

To make the ricotta: Set a large strainer over a deep bowl. Wet 2 layers of cheesecloth with water and use them to line the strainer. Set aside.

Pour the milk and cream into a large stainless-steel or enameled pot. Stir in the salt. Bring to a full boil over medium heat, stirring occasionally. Turn off the heat, stir in the vinegar, and let stand for 1 minute, or until the mixture curdles—it will separate into curds and whey.

Pour the mixture into the cheesecloth-lined sieve and allow it to drain into the bowl at room temperature, discarding the liquid in the bowl as needed, for 20 to 25 minutes—the longer you let the mixture drain, the thicker the ricotta will become. Season with salt and pepper. Use immediately or cover with plastic wrap and refrigerate for up to 4 days.

To make the hot honey: In a small bowl, combine the honey and hot sauce and microwave for 30 seconds. Stir to combine.

Assemble the dish by spreading the ricotta over the warm flatbread and drizzling with honey. Sprinkle with parsley and serve.

BIEROCKS WITH PEPPERED BEEF, GRILLED ONIONS, AND SHREDDED CHEESE

Serves 6 to 8

DOUGH

1½ Tbsp active dry yeast

7¼ cups all-purpose flour,
     plus additional as needed

¼ cup granulated sugar

1½ Tbsp garlic powder

1½ Tbsp kosher salt

¼ cup extra-virgin olive oil

continues ↗

Dust Bowl Brewing Company

TURLOCK, CALIFORNIA

The Pairing: Oktoberfest

These soft bread rolls are filled with peppered beef, grilled onions, and spicy pepper Jack beer cheese and will be gone just about as soon as they hit the table. They can be served as an appetizer or as a main course with a salad on the side. A bready and moderately hoppy Oktoberfest makes an ideal pairing, but also try these rolls with an Imperial West Coast IPA, which accentuates the spice.

To make the dough: In a medium bowl, combine the yeast and 3 cups of warm water, and let stand for 3 to 5 minutes to activate yeast.

In a large bowl, whisk together the flour, sugar, garlic powder, and salt. Add to the activated yeast mixture and whisk to combine. Add the olive oil and whisk until dough forms.

On a lightly floured surface, knead the dough for about 15 minutes, or until smooth. Add more flour to the dough as needed.

Oil a large bowl, put the dough in the bowl and let rise in a warm place for about 1 hour, or until doubled in size.

Oil a baking sheet. Divide the dough into 8 to 10 equal-sized pieces. Briefly knead the pieces then roll them into balls and arrange them on the prepared baking sheet. Let rest 10 minutes.

Dust Bowl Brewing Company
They say that great beer is born of hard times, and here at this brewing company, nestled in California's Central Valley, the portfolio of beers speaks to flavor and honest work. With multiple locations and a hearty distribution footprint, there are many opportunities for fans to find their big, hoppy IPAs and crisp lagers. This brewery takes pride in their appreciation for hard work, love of family, a hearty sense of humor, and a craving for new frontiers.

1 Tbsp extra-virgin olive oil

½ yellow onion, diced

2 lbs ground beef chuck

2 tsp chili powder

2 tsp kosher salt

1½ tsp freshly ground black
   pepper

½ tsp red pepper flakes

¼ tsp cayenne pepper

5 Tbsp all-purpose flour

1 cup lager

½ cup heavy cream

½ cup whole milk

⅓ cup shredded pepper Jack
   cheese

⅓ cup shredded Jack and
   Cheddar cheese, combined

Unsalted butter, melted
   (optional)

To make the filling: In a large skillet, heat the olive oil over medium heat. Add the onions and cook, stirring often, for about 5 minutes, or until translucent. Add the beef and cook, breaking it up with a wooden spoon, for 8 to 10 minutes, or until browned. Add the chili powder, salt, black pepper, red pepper, and cayenne and stir to combine. Add the flour and stir to incorporate. Add the beer and cook for 4 minutes then add the heavy cream, milk, and both cheeses and stir to incorporate. Remove from the heat and let cool.

Preheat the oven to 375°F. Flatten the dough balls into 7 to 8 in rounds. Put about ⅔ cup of the cooled beef mixture in the middle of each, shape the dough around the filling, and seal the dough by pinching the outer edges together, creating a roll. Place seam-side down on an oiled baking sheet. Brush with the melted butter (if using). Bake for 15 to 17 minutes, or until golden. Serve immediately.

SMOKED CHICKEN SALAD

Serves 6

¼ cup kosher salt
1 Tbsp granulated sugar
1 Tbsp whole black
  peppercorns
1 bay leaf
2 tsp mustard seeds
1 tsp apple cider vinegar
8 boneless chicken thighs
1 cup pecans
6 oz golden raisins
1 stalk celery, finely diced
¾ cup mayonnaise
½ medium yellow onion,
  finely diced
3 Tbsp chopped fresh dill
2 Tbsp Dijon mustard
2 tsp kosher salt

Perennial Artisan Ales

ST. LOUIS, MISSOURI

The Pairing: Autumn Lager

This recipe is a collaboration between Perennial co-owner Phil Wymore and Chef Kevin Willman. The smoked chicken can be served on a sandwich or by itself and paired with a seasonal autumn lager brewed with German pilsner and German Munich malt, a crisp lager with a nice bready backbone and a light cracker finish. "Unfiltered and crushable, this beer keeps you going through the fall months," says Wymore. This recipe requires a smoker for the best outcome, but the chicken thighs can be baked or grilled until thoroughly cooked through—they just won't have the same smoky flavor.

In a saucepan, bring the salt, sugar, peppercorns, bay leaf, and 4 cups of water to a simmer over medium-high heat. Continue simmering for about 10 minutes, or until the salt and sugar dissolve. Transfer to a large bowl or brine container and refrigerate for about 3 hours, or until it reaches about 40°F. Submerge the chicken in the brine, cover, and refrigerate for 5 to 8 hours.

In a small bowl, soak the mustard seeds in the apple cider vinegar for 5 to 8 hours or overnight.

Prepare the smoker and balance the fire between 225°F and 250°F. Use cherry wood chips or wood directed by the manufacturer of your smoker. Smoke the chicken thighs for 2 to 3 hours, or until the meat falls off the bone. Allow chicken to cool at room temperature then remove the meat from the bones, discarding any veins or skin.

In a medium bowl, combine the chicken, pecans, raisins, celery, mayonnaise, onion, dill, Dijon mustard, and salt. Drain the mustard seeds and add to the chicken mixture then fold to combine. Serve immediately or let sit for a day so the flavors can meld.

Perennial Artisan Ales

Shortly after it opened more than a decade ago, word started to get around in beer circles about the small St. Louis brewery that was making new-era American styles: ales of distinction with Belgian influence and some barrel-aged delights that were gobsmacking good. Perennial is now one of the most celebrated craft breweries in the country, with fans around the world and a commitment to pushing culinary boundaries both with their beer recipes and their relationships with chefs.

FALAFEL AND SPICED YOGURT

Serves 6

2 cups plain whole-milk
    yogurt
2 Tbsp cumin seeds
1 Tbsp coriander seeds
Zest and juice of 3 lemons
1 Tbsp paprika
½ tsp fine sea salt
½ onion, finely diced
2 garlic cloves, minced
2 Tbsp minced fresh flat-leaf
    parsley
1 Tbsp minced fresh cilantro
1 Tbsp kosher salt
One 15½ oz can chickpeas,
    drained and rinsed
¾ cup chickpea flour
Vegetable oil for frying

Fermentery Form
PHILADELPHIA, PENNSYLVANIA

The Pairing: Shandy

Aside from the yogurt and the falafel dough, which require some advance prep, this vegetarian recipe comes together quickly. Ethan Tripp of Fermentery Form says a shandy, particularly one with some extra spice like his Soft, a tart wit with orange juice and zest, coriander, and chamomile, pairs exceptionally well, especially with the spice of the yogurt.

Line a colander with cheesecloth and set over a medium bowl. Put the yogurt in the colander, cover the top with plastic wrap, and refrigerate for 8 to 10 hours, or until the liquid has drained and the yogurt has a thicker consistency.

In a small frying pan, toast the cumin and coriander seeds over low heat, tossing occasionally, for 5 to 7 minutes, or until fragrant. Transfer to a spice grinder and process until ground.

Transfer the drained yogurt to a clean medium bowl. Add the ground cumin and coriander along with the zest and juice of 1 lemon, the paprika, and the sea salt and stir to combine. Refrigerate until ready to use.

In a large bowl, combine the remaining lemon zest and juice, the onion, garlic, parsley, cilantro, and kosher salt and stir to combine. Transfer to a food processor, add the chickpeas, and pulse until the ingredients are combined and a dough forms. Transfer to a large mixing bowl, add the chickpea flour, and mix until uniform. Cover and refrigerate for 3 hours. (The dough can be refrigerated for up to 1 week.)

When ready to cook the falafel, shape the dough into small balls.

Fill a large Dutch oven, deep pot, or deep fryer with about 1 in of vegetable oil and heat to 350°F on a thermometer. Line a baking sheet with paper towels. Working in batches, fry the falafel balls for 3 to 5 minutes, or until golden brown. Transfer the falafels to the paper towel–lined baking sheet to drain. Fry the remaining falafel balls, adjusting the heat as needed to keep the oil at 350°F. Serve with the spiced yogurt.

Fermentery Form

Ethan Tripp was a home brewer before he went pro, but from early in his career he decided to take his time both with opening his own place (with friends, of course) and with the beers he wanted to make. He's succeeded in making deliberate beers that are rooted in tradition, but he isn't afraid to try new things or to use different ingredients to see how they develop. Time seems to move slowly at Fermentery Form, and that's by design. Ethan has had to learn patience, and that's something regular fans of his beer have had to practice as well, since not everything is always available when they might want it. It's not a brewery. That's important to note. So what is it, you might ask? Take the time to visit and experience it yourself.

SPICY CARAMEL PORK WITH EGG AND JASMINE RICE

Serves 6

¾ cup granulated sugar

4 to 5 lb pork butt roast, cut into cubes

10 whole red Thai chiles

5 garlic cloves, minced

3 scallions, thinly sliced and white and green parts separated

2 large shallots, minced

¼ cup fish sauce

½ tsp freshly ground black pepper

6 large eggs, hard boiled and peeled

3 cups cooked jasmine rice, for serving

American Solera Brewery

TULSA, OKLAHOMA

The Pairing: Bière de Garde

The name of this dish comes from the deep amber color the sugar turns while cooking, says its creator, Chef Bic Nguyen of Jackrabbit restaurant in Tulsa, Oklahoma. It's all about the spice, and a Bière de Garde is a perfect match. A Belgian- and French-influenced beer, Bière de Garde has moderate alcohol, some hop spice, and a biscuity, toasted malt profile that can, at times, offer a caramel-like sweetness.

In a large saucepan, cook the sugar without stirring over medium heat for 5 to 7 minutes, or until it turns a light brown caramel color. Add the pork, Thai chiles, garlic, the white parts of the scallions, shallots, fish sauce, and pepper and stir to combine. Turn the heat to low and bring to a simmer. Continue simmering, stirring occasionally, for 90 minutes, or until pork is fork tender.

About 10 minutes before the pork is done cooking, add the hard-boiled eggs and gently stir to coat them in the sauce, being careful not to break the eggs. When done, divide the pork, sauce, and jasmine rice between 6 bowls. Cut the eggs in half and add 2 halves to each bowl. Sprinkle with scallion greens and serve.

American Solera Brewery

By the time Chase and Erica Healey opened American Solera, Chase had cut his teeth at several other breweries and had garnered praise and attention for his wood-aged beers. Once the couple had their own space, filled with barrels and using recipes of all kinds, American Solera created some of the country's finest wild ales. It still does so but has also kept up with the changing times. Now, alongside the brewery's blended farmhouse ales, you'll find hard seltzers and pilsners, made with the same care and attention to detail, but a reminder that beer is a constantly evolving space.

BEEF CHEEK PIE WITH STILTON BLUE CHEESE

Serves 6 to 8

5 lbs beef cheeks, trimmed and cut into 1½ in chunks
Kosher salt and freshly ground black pepper
3 large yellow onions
½ cup olive oil
3 garlic cloves, peeled and crushed
2 carrots, roughly chopped
2 celery stalks, roughly chopped
2 cups Eisbock
3 cups chicken broth
2 bay leaves
1 sprig fresh rosemary
1 sprig fresh thyme
1 cup HP Sauce or steak sauce
1 lb Stilton, crumbled
8 sheets store-bought puff pastry, thawed if frozen
1 large egg, lightly beaten

Carton Brewing Company

ATLANTIC HIGHLANDS, NEW JERSEY

The Pairing: Eisbock

Eisbocks are a pleasure and an especially great way to link a hearty last course to dessert. They are sweet and rich, but the great ones are never cloying—instead, they flit among warm, fruity, thick, and roasty. Carton Brewing, working with Chef James Avery, created this pairing in which unctuous beef cheeks and funky Stilton, wrapped in a buttery warm package, draw deeply on the Eisbock's fruitiness. A simple arugula salad makes a great side for this decadent main.

Preheat the oven to 375°F.

Season the beef cheeks with salt and pepper. Thinly slice 2 of the onions and roughly chop the third onion.

Heat ¼ cup of the olive oil in a Dutch oven over medium-high heat. Working in batches, add the beef cheeks and cook, turning as needed, for 6 to 8 minutes, or until browned on all sides. Transfer to a plate and set aside.

Add the garlic, carrots, celery, and the roughly chopped onion to the Dutch oven and cook over medium-high heat for 8 to 10 minutes, or until golden. Add the beer and cook for 5 to 7 minutes, or until reduced by half. Return the beef cheeks to pan, along with chicken broth, 1 of the bay leaves, the rosemary, and the thyme and bring to a boil. Boil for 1 minute then cover the Dutch oven, transfer to the oven, and cook for about 2½ hours, or until the beef is very tender. Transfer the beef cheeks to a cutting board and let cool then shred the meat into bite-size pieces.

Carton Brewing Company

When this brewery launched a decade ago, among the first in a wave of next-generation Garden State breweries, it introduced beers with complex culinary approaches that were accessible for every palate. Playing in traditional spaces with offbeat ingredients and techniques, Carton Brewing quickly gained a reputation for pushing the envelope. Its flagship beer, Boat, is a hazy pale ale that is delicate and refreshing yet still somehow sturdy enough to be a proper session beer at 4.2 percent abv. From the Jersey Shore to your glass, Carton is a brewery with soul and style.

Strain the sauce through a fine-mesh strainer into a bowl; discard the solids. Add the shredded beef to the sauce. Turn the oven down to 350°F.

Meanwhile, in a large skillet, heat the remaining olive oil over medium heat. Add the 2 sliced onions and the remaining bay leaf and cook, stirring occasionally, for about 45 minutes, or until the onions are caramelized. Add the HP sauce and cook, stirring occasionally, for 2 to 3 minutes, or until all the sauce is evaporated. Add to the beef mixture and stir to combine.

Pour the beef mixture into a 2 qt oval or 9 x 13 in baking dish and sprinkle the Stilton cheese crumbles on top. Following the instructions on the package for handling, arrange the puff pastry over the filling, trimming any excess. Use a fork to press the pastry into the edges of the baking dish. Brush the top of the pastry with the beaten egg and cut three slits in the surface. Bake for about 1 hour and 15 minutes, or until the pastry is golden brown and the filling is bubbling. Allow to cool for 10 minutes before serving.

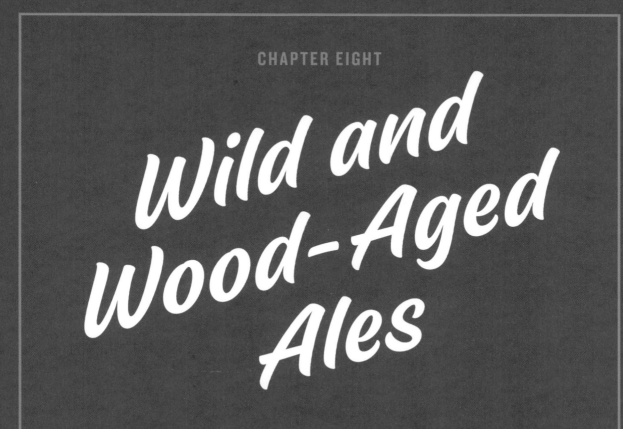

Wild and Wood-Aged Ales

While two distinct styles of beer, there is a lot of overlap between wood-aged beers and wild ales. Though once rarities, reserved for special occasions like brewery anniversaries or holiday releases, barrel-aged beers of all kinds have become more commonplace. Even the smallest of breweries boast a "barrel program" that might consist of a few beers hanging out in wood in the corner. Other, larger breweries have gone all-in on barrel programs, housing thousands of barrels in expansive warehouses.

Oak is the primary wood that brewers use, and depending on the char and whether or not it has been used for something previously, you can get notes of vanilla, toasted coconut, and a woody, tea-like tannin flavor that peeks through the base beer style. Many beers are aged on simple wood, but more and more, brewers looking to expand their horizons are using specialty woods that can infuse cedar or spice into a beer.

Some beers are aged in wine or spirits barrels to impart the flavors of those beverages into the beers. Bourbon barrels are the most common for spirit barrels, but beers aged in tequila, scotch, and rum barrels all show up on tap lists from time to time. Still, for all the fun in chasing down beers that have been aged in prized spirits barrels, there is also a return to tradition by some brewers who are simply using fresh, untreated barrels to age beers, letting the wood become a full expression in the beer.

Wine barrels, filled with tannins and aromas from grapes, usually contain flavors that complement beer styles like dark ales.

Wild ales are beers that are fermented by naturally ambient yeast and bacteria. One of the best ways to capture those microbes is by using a coolship. This is an open-to-air vessel in which, as the wort cools, it is exposed to local yeast and bacteria that inoculate the beer and begins the fermentation process. After a day or so, the beer is collected and drained into a fermentation vessel, which is sometimes stainless-steel but more often made of wood.

Brettanomyces is a common naturally occurring yeast, although there are other strains that can inoculate beer. Some breweries are located in wooded areas, while others are along city train lines or in the heart of a metropolitan area. Each location is different, and the various ambient yeasts and bacteria help provide a sense of place through the taste of beer. Some breweries even use mobile coolships that can be filled with wort from the brewhouse and taken anywhere from the shores of lakes to the middle of vast fields—or even just a parking lot adjacent to the brewery.

Brettanomyces and *Lactobacillus*, a probiotic bacteria, along with other specialty yeast strains or spontaneous fermentation, make for a still largely unknown beer universe and can impart flavors of pepper, spice, leather, tobacco, and earth. Fruits like peach, cherry, and raspberry are a popular addition to these beers, and most are bottle conditioned, meaning yeast or bacteria are added before a bottle is capped or corked. Thanks to *Brettanomyces*, many of these beers are suited to age over time.

Because many wild ales and wood-aged beers are on the heavier side, you need assertive dishes that won't be completely rolled over by the beer. There are fun pairings, including sea salt–caramel vanilla-bean ice cream, roasted meats, breakfast hash, and herb-infused potatoes, that can really make stellar companions. For robust barrel-aged beers, especially imperial stouts, look to ingredients like blue cheese to help absorb some of the flavor. No longer just for special occasions, barrel-aged beers are ready to open whenever the mood strikes. The style should also get closer consideration for everyday food pairing.

JOHNNY-CAKES WITH JONAH CRAB

Serves 4

JOHNNYCAKES
1 cup whole milk
2 cups fine cornmeal
1 tsp fine sea salt
1 Tbsp unsalted butter
Vegetable oil

JONAH CRAB
2 Tbsp finely chopped chives
1 Tbsp finely diced celery, plus
    leaves, reserved for serving
1 tsp fine sea salt
2 Tbsp extra-virgin olive oil
1 Tbsp fresh lemon juice
1 Tbsp apple cider vinegar
1 Tbsp maple syrup
8 oz Jonah crabmeat
Fine sea salt and freshly
    ground black pepper

LEMON CRÈME FRAÎCHE
¼ cup crème fraîche
1 tsp lemon zest
2 tsp lemon juice
½ tsp salt

Trillium Brewing
CANTON, MASSACHUSETTS

The Pairing: American Wild Ale or Oenobier

These cornmeal flatbreads, created by Trillium's executive chef, Thomas Park, are a perfect base for the tangy, sweet, and savory crab. Bright, lemony crème fraîche brings the whole dish together. Brunch has never been so good, especially when paired with an American wild ale, like Trillium's Dogtooth Violet. This also pairs well with Oenobier, a style that fuses wine making, beer making, and their respective ingredients.

To make the johnnycakes: In a small saucepan, bring the milk and ½ cup of water to boil over medium-high heat. Whisk in the cornmeal and salt. Remove from the heat, add the butter, and whisk until fully melted. Let stand, stirring occasionally, until fully cooled.

In a large cast-iron or nonstick pan, heat a thin layer of vegetable oil over medium-high heat. Spoon about 2 Tbsp of the cooled batter into the pan and spread into circles about ¼ to ½ in thick. Cook, flipping as needed, for 2 to 3 minutes per side, or until browned. Transfer to a plate while you cook the remaining batter.

To make the Jonah crab: In a small bowl, combine the chives, celery, and salt. Let stand for 5 minutes then add the olive oil, lemon juice, apple cider vinegar, and maple syrup, and mix until combined. Gently fold in the crab and season with salt and pepper.

To make the lemon crème fraîche: In a small bowl, combine the crème fraîche with the lemon zest and juice. Season with salt.

Place the johnnycakes on a serving plate or platter and spoon the crab mixture on top of each one. Place a small dollop of crème fraîche on top of each and sprinkle with the celery leaves.

Trillium Brewing

Named after the Massachusetts state flower, this brewery has been blossoming since it opened its doors in 2013. With multiple locations in the state, including a celebrated brewpub on the Boston waterfront and a working farm in Connecticut, Trillium quickly gained fame for its New England–style IPAs, but those in the know will tell you the real genius is in their wild and experimental ales. The line at Trillium always forms early and goes long. Plan your visit accordingly.

KALE CAESAR SALAD WITH MISO AND SHRIMP

Serves 4

SHRIMP
6 to 8 large shrimp, deveined
    and cleaned
1 Tbsp extra-virgin olive oil
1 Tbsp grated garlic
Fine sea salt
1 Tbsp canola oil

DRESSING
½ cup light mayonnaise
2 Tbsp freshly grated
    Parmesan cheese
2 Tbsp extra-virgin olive oil
2 Tbsp white miso paste
1 Tbsp Dijon mustard
1 Tbsp rice vinegar
1 garlic clove, grated
1 anchovy fillet or 1 Tbsp
    anchovy paste
Fine sea salt and freshly
    ground black pepper

SALAD
5 or 6 large sprigs curly kale,
    stemmed and chopped
¼ cup thinly sliced radicchio
½ cup croutons
Shaved Parmesan cheese

Jester King Brewery
AUSTIN, TEXAS

The Pairing: Farmhouse Ale

Snörkel, Jester King Brewery's farmhouse ale, is brewed with alderwood smoked sea salt and oyster mushrooms, and pairs wonderfully with this salad. Both feature strong umami profiles, while staying light and refreshing as a pairing. Other spontaneous ales, or even a Gose or mushroom-accented IPA, would also bring out the best in this salad, which can be served with or without the shrimp.

To make the shrimp: Pat the shrimp dry with a paper towel then put in a small bowl, add the olive oil, garlic, and salt, and toss to coat. In a large skillet, heat the canola oil over high heat until wisps of smoke appear. Add the shrimp and cook until opaque and cooked through, about 2 minutes per side. Remove from the pan and set aside.

To make the dressing: In a blender or food processor, combine the mayonnaise, Parmesan cheese, olive oil, miso paste, Dijon mustard, rice vinegar, garlic, and anchovy. Blend until smooth then season with salt and pepper.

To make the salad: Put the kale in a large bowl, add the dressing, and toss until the leaves are lightly coated. Top with the radicchio, croutons, and shrimp. Sprinkle with Parmesan shavings and serve immediately.

Jester King Brewery
This brewery, on the outskirts of Austin, is the stuff of legend among many drinkers and was driven to heights of popularity by the wild and spontaneous beer that founder Jeffrey Stuffings and his brewers have produced over the years. They've also adapted to the times and now have a clean fermentation program. There's even a wine program in the works.

BRAISED PORK BELLY

Beachwood BBQ + Brewing + Blendery

LONG BEACH, CALIFORNIA

The Pairing: Belgian-Style Sour Ale

Pork belly has become a go-to dish for brewery restaurants that want to bring rich flavor to the plate while still allowing the beer to shine through in the glass. This recipe relies on time to let the flavors develop. It can be served with a variety of sides, or even shredded for a sandwich. Pair it with a fruited Belgian-style sour ale, like Beachwood Blendery's Funk Yeah series, where a little bit of sweetness goes a long way.

Serves 6 to 8

BRINE

1 cup caraway seeds
2 cups apple cider vinegar
1 cup kosher salt
1 cup packed dark brown
   sugar
6 garlic cloves, crushed
3 Tbsp fennel seeds
3 Tbsp whole black
   peppercorns
3 Tbsp coriander seeds

PORK

2 lbs pork belly
2 Tbsp canola oil
1 carrot, chopped
1 celery stalk, chopped
1 onion, chopped
4 garlic cloves, crushed
6 sprigs fresh thyme
3 Tbsp caraway seeds, toasted
4 cups apple cider vinegar
4 cups chicken broth

To make the brine: In a large skillet, toast the caraway seeds over low heat for 5 minutes, or until fragrant. Let the seeds cool then grind in a spice grinder. Transfer to a large plastic container and add the apple cider vinegar, salt, brown sugar, garlic, fennel, peppercorns, coriander, and 4 cups of water.

To make the pork: Add the pork to the brine, cover, and refrigerate for 24 hours.

Preheat the oven to 300°F. Remove the pork belly from the brine and pat dry with paper towels. Season the pork belly on both sides with salt and pepper.

In a large Dutch oven, heat the canola oil over medium-high heat. Add the pork and cook, turning as needed, for 10 minutes, or until brown on all sides. Transfer to a plate. Add the carrot, celery, onion, garlic, thyme, and toasted caraway seeds to the pan and cook, stirring occasionally, for about 5 minutes, or until the vegetables are caramelized and the onion is translucent. Return the pork belly to the pan, skin side up. Pour in the apple cider vinegar and enough broth to cover most of the meat, leaving the top exposed. Bring to a boil then cover, transfer to the oven, and cook for about 2 hours, or until the pork belly is very tender. Cool the pork belly in its braising liquid then refrigerate, covered, overnight.

When ready to serve, preheat the oven to 300°F. Scrape off and discard excess fat from the braising liquid. Remove the pork from the braising liquid and discard any loose gelatin. Cut the pork into serving pieces and place in a wide, ovenproof sauté pan. Bring the braising liquid to a boil and continue boiling until reduced by about two-thirds or until it coats the back of a spoon. Strain the braising liquid through a fine-mesh strainer into a bowl; discard the solids. Pour just enough of the strained liquid over the pork to cover it halfway and transfer to the oven. Cook, basting occasionally, for about 25 minutes, or until warmed through. Serve the pork topped with the sauce.

Beachwood BBQ + Brewing + Blendery

There is a sense of anticipation before visiting one of Beachwood's locations in southern California. Even for a quick trip, there's a wonder about new beers on tap or specials from the kitchen. Or maybe it's just the desire for some familiar comfort food and drink. This brewery has garnered accolades for all the right reasons and continues to bring new beer fans into the fold through hospitality and nourishment. The Blendery is dedicated to producing beers inspired by the Belgian lambic and gueuze traditions.

GRILLED CAULIFLOWER STEAKS WITH BUTTERNUT SQUASH PURÉE

Serves 4

CAULIFLOWER

Regular or vegan mayonnaise, for cooking

1 large head cauliflower, cut crosswise into four to five 1½ in thick steaks

¼ cup homemade or store-bought barbecue rub

PICKLED RADISHES

1 bunch radishes, thinly sliced on a mandoline slicer

½ cup apple cider vinegar

½ cup kosher salt

3 dried chiles (optional)

PURÉE

1 medium butternut squash, halved lengthwise and seeded

¾ cup (1½ sticks) unsalted butter or ¾ cup plant-based spread

2 Tbsp maple syrup

½ tsp kosher salt

¼ tsp freshly grated nutmeg

continues ↗

Revolution Brewing

CHICAGO, ILLINOIS

The Pairing: Barrel-Aged Barleywine

Prior to founding Revolution Brewing, Josh Deth owned a vegetarian restaurant that featured fresh, in-season ingredients from local producers before it was a trend. When pairing a barrel-aged barleywine, like the brewery's Straight Jacket, the impulse is to go with bold barbecue-inflected flavors, but you don't actually need a slab of beef. The sweetness of this squash purée matches the toffee-like notes in an aged barleywine, while the spices and sear add contrast and provide depth in the same way the barrel brings new dimensions to the beer. If you're feeling ambitious, make your own rub with equal parts smoked sweet paprika and brown sugar mixed with ⅔ the amount of salt and ½₀ of garlic powder, onion powder, dry mustard, black pepper, and coriander seed.

To make the cauliflower: Spread the mayonnaise evenly on both sides of the cauliflower steaks, and then coat with the rub. Refrigerate until ready to grill.

To make the pickled radishes: Pack the sliced radishes in a qt-sized jar.

In a nonreactive saucepan, bring the apple cider vinegar, kosher salt, chiles (if using), and ¼ cup of water to a boil over high heat, stirring to combine. Pour over the radishes and seal the jar tightly. The pickles can be stored at refrigerated for up to a week.

To make the butternut squash purée: Preheat the oven to 375°F. Line a baking sheet with parchment paper.

Arrange the butternut squash, cut-side down, on the prepared baking sheet and bake for 45 minutes, or until fork-tender. Cut into small pieces

> ### Revolution Brewing
> *There is something for everyone at this venerable Chicago brewpub and brewery tasting room. With its assertive hoppy ales to Belgian-inspired ales, pilsners, and more, it is billed as the largest "independently owned" brewery in the city and it's made a positive national name for itself. This reputation has been helped by Revolution's expansive wood- and barrel-aged beer collection that racks up medals, intrigues palates, delights senses, and often makes for a rough morning after.*

2 Tbsp grapeseed or other cooking oil

1 lb collard greens, stemmed and chopped

2 tsp apple cider vinegar

1 tsp kosher salt

and transfer to a large bowl. Add the butter, maple syrup, kosher salt, and nutmeg. Using an immersion blender, purée until smooth. Cover and keep warm.

To make the collards: In a large skillet, heat the grapeseed oil over medium-high heat. Add the collards, tossing to coat in the oil then add ½ cup of water, cover, and cook for 6 minutes, or until greens are wilted. Uncover the pan then add the vinegar and kosher salt. Remove from the heat and keep warm.

Heat a grill or griddle to medium. Grill the cauliflower steaks, flipping once, for 4 to 5 minutes per side, or until starting to brown. Serve the cauliflower steaks with the butternut squash purée, collard greens, and pickled radishes.

ZEPPOLE

Serves 6 to 8

4 cups all-purpose flour

½ cup granulated sugar

2 Tbsp baking soda

1½ cups whole milk ricotta
 cheese

8 large eggs

2 Tbsp pure vanilla extract
 or paste

1 cup fresh berries or ¼ cup
 bittersweet chocolate
 chips (optional)

2 qt canola or other neutral
 cooking oil

Confectioners' sugar

Fernson Brewing Company

SIOUX FALLS, SOUTH DAKOTA

The Pairing: Farmhouse Ale

This traditional fried pastry would pair with any number of sweet beers, including stouts, but a rustic farmhouse ale—wheat-forward, funky, and spicy—brings out some of the richness in the ricotta, while lending a bready note to the flour.

In a large bowl, whisk together the flour, granulated sugar, and baking soda. Add the ricotta, eggs, and vanilla and stir until combined into a batter. Add the fresh berries or chocolate chips (if using) or keep plain.

Fill a large Dutch oven, deep pot, or deep fryer with 2 in of canola oil and heat to 350°F on a thermometer. Line a baking sheet with paper towels. Working in batches, use a tablespoon to scoop out the batter and drop into the oil, creating little balls. Fry, turning occasionally, for 4 minutes, or until evenly browned all over. Use a slotted spoon to transfer to the prepared baking sheet to drain briefly. Fry the remaining zeppole, adjusting the heat as needed to keep the oil at 350°F. Generously dust with confectioners' sugar and serve immediately.

Fernson Brewing Company
A real sense of community surrounds this growing South Dakota brewery. One of the first craft breweries to open in the state, Fernson has worked to promote small batch beer and educate their neighbors about it. Through two taprooms and a growing distribution footprint they have worked tirelessly to bring the best flavors to thirsty drinkers.

WILD ALE SORBET

Makes 3 cups

2 cups coolship or wild ale
¾ cup granulated sugar
Fresh fruit, for serving
(optional)

The Pairing: Coolship Ale

Although you can make a beer sorbet with any kind of beer, most people opt for something sweet or fruit forward. But several years ago, at a beer dinner at the Ruck, a great beer bar in Troy, New York, I was served a sorbet made with a coolship ale from Allagash Brewing. The spontaneously fermented ale, with its funk, wild microbes, and tangy nature, was livened up with the additional sugar and near-freezing sorbet-making process. Now, when I make a beer sorbet, I can't imagine any other style working better.

Put the beer in a medium bowl and stir several times to release some carbonation. Refrigerate for 30 minutes.

In a medium saucepan, combine the sugar and 1 cup of water and bring to a simmer over medium heat, stirring to dissolve the sugar and create a simple syrup. Remove from the heat and refrigerate until cool, about 2 hours.

Put a container large enough to hold 3 cups of sorbet into the freezer.

Add the cold simple syrup to the cold beer then pour into an ice cream maker and process according to the manufacturer's instructions for about 30 minutes, or until thick. Transfer to the prepared container and freeze for at least 3 hours. Serve with fresh fruit (if using) and a glass of coolship or wild ale.

PORTER ICE CREAM

Makes ½ gallon

¾ cup half-and-half
3 cups heavy cream
4 large eggs
½ cup D180 candi syrup, or similar candi syrup
1 Tbsp gelatin or agar-agar
¾ cup Russian River Porter or similar
1½ cups granulated sugar
½ tsp fine sea salt
1 tsp vanilla extract

Russian River Brewing Company

WINDSOR, CALIFORNIA

The Pairing: Wine Barrel–Aged Porter

This house favorite of Vinnie and Natalie Cilurzo calls for Russian River porter, but any locally made porter works in a pinch. Beer ice cream, when made well, still imparts carbonation, adding an extra layer of mouthfeel to each bite. Pair with a red wine barrel–aged porter like Russian River's Propitiation. The roast-forward porter takes on a slight tart and sour note from the barrel and will help cut through the fullness of the dairy. This recipe calls for candi syrup, a sugar syrup used in making Belgian-style ales; it can be purchased online or in home-brewing stores. The alcohol in the beer will not fully freeze, so using gelatin is necessary. A vegetarian alternative is agar-agar. Note that this recipe requires the use of a sous vide machine in addition to an ice-cream maker.

Preheat a sous vide machine to 160°F. In a mixing bowl combine half-and-half, heavy cream, eggs, and candi syrup, and mix until fully combined. Transfer to an airtight sous vide bag and cook for 30 minutes to heat ingredients through without scrambling the eggs. Remove the bag from the sous vide machine then strain the ice cream mixture through a fine-mesh strainer set over a bowl. Slowly sprinkle the gelatin over the ice cream mixture and use an immersion blender (or whisk) to fully incorporate.

Pour the beer between 2 pint glasses about 10 times to remove some of its carbonation.

Add beer, sugar, salt, and vanilla extract to the custard, and stir to combine. Cover bowl and place in the refrigerator for at least 8 hours to cool and set.

Transfer the mixture to the cannister of your ice cream maker and churn according to the manufacturer's instructions until thick. Freeze overnight before serving.

Russian River Brewing Company

Once a year, beer fans flock to northern California for the release of Pliny the Younger, the triple IPA from this beloved craft brewery. While that gets a lot of attention, their more moderate, year-round IPAs, including Pliny the Elder and Blind Pig, are world-class examples of the styles and cult favorites of beer drinkers. With a deep appreciation for wine, they helped usher in an era of beers aged in former wine barrels, creating a line of wild beers that explore the intersection of wood, grapes, malt, and hops.

Mix Pack

The modern beer industry has become about choice and variety. There are more than a dozen different styles of IPA, and even more for lager. There are subcategories to just about every style of beer that exists, often playing on regional beer making preferences.

With the emergence of new hop varieties every year, new flavors are constantly being introduced to beer, and brewers are finding new ingredients to add to their recipes. Because of this, styles as we once knew them have begun to change. Brewers are also melding styles (black Kölsch comes to mind as one that sent traditional brewmasters into a tizzy) and brewing without regard for established recipes. This can lead to confusion on labels, but ultimately, it's our taste buds that decide if a beer works or not.

Still, there are guidelines that exist through the Beer Judge Certification Program and the Brewers Association, which runs the annual Great American Beer Festival competition, and they offer up specifics of what a certain style *should* taste like. These are good resources for the curious beer drinker.

Choice is a good thing but can also be overwhelming. The good news is that with beer, you don't have to make a lifelong commitment. If you see a beer that looks appealing, give it a try. If you don't like it, move on. It's important to note that no two beers are alike and that style representations can vary wildly from one brewery to another. So, if a red ale at one brewery doesn't land on your palate the right way, give another brewery's version a shot. If you still don't love it after a few tries, it's likely that the style isn't for you, and that's okay. There are plenty of other styles to discover.

Tasting through styles is an adventure, and it's personal. A good adage is: Never yuck someone else's yum. Like what you like, and don't like what you don't. When looking at beer descriptions, try to visualize food pairings. If something is sweet, find a contrast. If it has moderate acidity, think about a food that can cut through that. Does a honey beer make you think of ham? Try that pairing. A lemon-accented beer paired with fish? That makes sense. Over time, we develop personal tastes and preferred combinations, but taking a beat to think about what a brewer has added to a beer or the flavors of the main ingredients can quickly create a pairing in your mind.

Here are some recipes that pair with outlying styles—from cream ales and Scotch ales to Zwickelbiers—that you are likely to encounter on tap or on shelves and that should be a part of any delicious beer dinner.

PRETZEL BITES

Serves 6 to 8

1 cup amber ale
1 Tbsp raw cane sugar
2 tsp kosher salt, plus more
  for dusting the pretzels
1¼ tsp active dry yeast
4 Tbsp (½ stick) unsalted
  butter, cut into small
  pieces
4 cups all-purpose flour
⅔ cup baking soda
1 large egg white

No need for twists or knots—this easy-to-make handheld snack has all the familiar flavors of a giant pretzel but is easier to share with friends. Pair with a spicy rye ale or a caramel malt-forward amber ale that has light fruity notes. Serve with Garlic Cheese Spread and Porter Mustard (following recipe).

In a medium saucepan, bring the beer and ½ cup water to a simmer over low heat. Transfer to the bowl of a stand mixer. Add the sugar, salt, and yeast and let stand for 5 minutes, or until slightly foamy. With the mixer on low and using the dough hook attachment, gradually add the butter until combined and then add the flour. Continue mixing, gradually increasing the speed, for about 5 minutes, or until a dough forms.

Lightly oil a large bowl and put the dough inside. Cover the bowl with plastic wrap and let rest for 1 hour at room temperature, or until doubled in size.

Preheat the oven to 400°F. Line a baking sheet with parchment paper.

In a medium saucepan, combine the baking soda and 3 qt of water. Bring to a boil over high heat.

In a small bowl, whisk the egg white with 1 Tbsp of water to create an egg wash.

On a lightly oiled surface, roll out the dough in a rope shape until about ¾ in thick. Cut into 1 in pieces and then roll each one into a ball.

Working in batches, carefully add a few balls of dough to the boiling water and cook for 1 minute. Use a slotted spoon to carefully remove the balls from the boiling water. Place on the prepared baking sheet and brush pretzel bites in egg wash and dust with salt. Repeat with the remaining dough balls, adjusting the heat as needed to keep the water boiling. Bake for 10 minutes, or until golden brown. Serve hot.

GARLIC CHEESE SPREAD AND PORTER MUSTARD

Makes 3 cups

MUSTARD

½ cup black mustard seeds
½ cup yellow mustard seeds
1½ cups malt vinegar
2 cups porter
5 Tbsp honey
½ cup dark brown sugar
2 teaspoons fine sea salt
2 teaspoons ground allspice
¾ teaspoon turmeric
1 cup dry ground mustard

SPREAD

8 oz extra-sharp Cheddar
    cheese, shredded
8 oz cream cheese, at room
    temperature
2 tsp powdered ranch dressing
    mix
1½ tsp garlic powder
½ tsp dried parsley
¼ cup Vienna lager, plus
    additional as needed

Frog Alley Brewing Co.

SCHENECTADY, NEW YORK

Rich Michaels, brewmaster at Frog Alley Brewing Co., shared these recipes from his home kitchen. They are wonderful accompaniments to the easy-to-make-at-home Pretzel Bites (previous recipe).

To make the mustard: In a medium bowl, combine the black and yellow mustard seeds, the vinegar, and 1½ cups of the beer. Cover and refrigerate overnight.

In a medium saucepan, bring the remaining ½ cup of the beer (it can be open and refrigerated overnight) and the honey, brown sugar, salt, allspice, and turmeric to a boil over high heat. Remove from the heat, transfer to a blender, and let cool. Add the ground mustard, along with the mustard seeds and their soaking liquid, and blend until smooth. Transfer to a glass jar, seal tightly, and refrigerate overnight and for up to 3 months.

To make the spread: In a large bowl, combine the Cheddar cheese, cream cheese, ranch dressing mix, garlic powder, and parsley. Using a handheld mixer, beat on low until combined. Slowly add the beer and mix on high speed until smooth. For a thinner spread, gradually add more beer. Cover and refrigerate until ready to use and for up to 2 weeks; the spread will thicken when chilled.

Frog Alley Brewing Co.

This modern brewery—named after a baseball team that once played in New York's capital region and in 1903 saw all its players arrested for violating blue laws—has been turning out flavorful traditional ales and lagers for several years under the watchful eye of master brewer Rich Michaels. In a gleaming facility that inspires awe from professional brewers and drinkers alike, the team here gives it their best effort and leaves it all on the field.

MANGO AND BEET SALAD

Serves 4

2 medium beets, trimmed and scrubbed
1 Tbsp extra-virgin olive oil
Juice of 1 lime
1 garlic clove, crushed and peeled
2 ripe Champagne mangoes, peeled, halved, and cut into ⅛ in slices
¼ cup chopped fennel fronds

Athletic Brewing Co.

STRATFORD, CONNECTICUT

The Pairing: Nonalcoholic Golden Ale

Healthy with healthy is always a good pairing, and this salad created by John Walker, cofounder and head brewer of Athletic Brewing Co., is just what's called for on a detox day—or any day. It's very refreshing and vibrant yet amazingly rich, deep, and complex. A nonalcoholic golden ale, especially Athletic Brewing's Upside Dawn, offers a clean malt profile, along with pine and citrusy hops that complement the earthiness of the salad, while also accentuating and balancing its sweetness. This is a stunner of a dish, as the beet bleeds into the mango, creating a beautiful rainbow effect.

Preheat the oven to 350°F.

Wrap the beets in foil and roast directly on the oven rack for about 1 hour, or until tender. Remove the foil then carefully remove the skins. Let the beets cool to room temperature then cut into rounds.

In a medium bowl, whisk together the olive oil and lime juice until emulsified. Add the garlic and let stand for 5 minutes then remove and discard the garlic. Add the mangoes and toss to coat.

On a serving platter or plate, arrange the beet and mango slices in alternating layers with each one peeking out from the other to showcase their contrasting colors. Top with fennel and drizzle with the remaining lime and olive oil mixture. Serve immediately.

Athletic Brewing Co.
Athletic Brewing Co. is changing the way American drinkers think about nonalcoholic beer. The brewery, with locations in Connecticut and California, has introduced familiar styles—from IPAs to stouts to golden ales and more—that start at 50 calories and are alcohol free. As generations of drinkers get older and think about long-term health, there's now an option to keep heads clear and drink a beer anytime, anywhere.

LONZINO AND AGED GOUDA SALAD

Serves 4

VINAIGRETTE

2 preserved lemons
½ cup fresh lemon juice (from
    2 to 3 lemons)
½ shallot, finely chopped
2 Tbsp fresh thyme
2 Tbsp sherry vinegar
1 Tbsp Dijon mustard
1 tsp ground coriander
1 clove finely chopped garlic
3 cups extra-virgin olive oil
3 Tbsp mustard oil
Fine sea salt and freshly ground
    black pepper

SALAD

6 cups Bloomsdale or savoy
    spinach
2 cups thinly shaved radicchio,
    preferably Treviso
1 small sweet onion, thinly shaved
Fine sea salt and fresh ground
    black pepper
5 oz Lonzino or prosciutto, thinly
    shaved
2 oz aged Gouda, preferably
    3 to 5 years, thinly shaved
½ cup quartered jarred artichokes,
    lightly grilled
¼ cup roughly chopped toasted
    pistachios

Pure Project
SAN DIEGO, CALIFORNIA

The Pairing: Unfiltered Pilsner

There is a lot of kick to this salad, which brings together earthy and spicy greens, cured salty pork loin, and aged cheese. It is a meal in itself, and this recipe from San Diego caterers MIHO paired with a Zwickelbier—an unfiltered pilsner—totally sings. Rich pilsner malt and a hop profile of sweet spice and dried flowers, like what you'll find in Pure Project's Rain, add an herbal complexity to each bite. You'll have more than enough vinaigrette, but it's versatile and keeps for a month.

To make the vinaigrette: Remove the flesh from the preserved lemons and reserve for another use. Chop the rinds and place in a food processor. Add the lemon juice, shallots, thyme, sherry vinegar, Dijon mustard, coriander, and garlic and blend until smooth. With the food processor on, slowly add the olive oil and mustard oil and blend to combine. Season with salt and pepper. The vinaigrette can be refrigerated in an airtight container for up to 1 month.

To make the salad: In a large bowl, gently toss the spinach, radicchio, and sweet onion until well combined. Drizzle with ¼ cup of the vinaigrette, season with salt and pepper, and gently toss again.

Divide the greens among plates. Top with the Lonzino, Gouda, artichokes, and pistachios and serve.

Pure Project

In a beer city where hops have long ruled, Pure Project has emerged as a brewery incubator that pushes the limits of style, while also bringing new recipes to the forefront. With a robust mixed culture program and some of the haziest IPAs you can find, this brewery, which is part of the 1% for the Planet environmental network, still finds time for a few traditional recipes, pilsners included.

LOUISIANA SHRIMP AND SAUSAGE STEW

Serves 6 to 8

1 Tbsp olive oil
1 red bell pepper, chopped
½ lb okra, sliced
½ lb asparagus, trimmed and chopped
1 jalapeño, seeded and diced
2 Tbsp Old Bay seasoning
1 tsp garlic powder
1 tsp fine sea salt
1 tsp freshly ground black pepper
1 qt chicken stock
1 lb andouille sausage, sliced
1 lb cleaned and peeled shrimp
¼ lb spinach

St. Elmo Brewing Co.

AUSTIN, TEXAS

The Pairing: Kölsch

This is a quick stew that can be pulled together in the time it takes to drink a proper pint of lager. St. Elmo cofounder Tim Bullock created this milder version, but notes that if onions and garlic are your jam, adding those ingredients to the pot will kick up the flavor. A light and snappy Kölsch offers balance to the meaty sausage and won't overwhelm the spices.

In a large stockpot, heat the olive oil over medium heat until shimmering. Add the bell pepper, okra, asparagus, and jalapeño and sauté, stirring occasionally, for 7 minutes, or until softened. Add the Old Bay seasoning, garlic powder, salt, and pepper, stir to combine, and cook for 1 minute.

Turn the heat to high, add the chicken stock and 1 cup of water, and bring to a boil. Turn the heat to medium-low and simmer for 10 minutes.

Meanwhile, in a large skillet, fry the sausage over medium heat, turning frequently, for about 10 minutes, or until firm. Add the cooked sausage, along with the shrimp and spinach, to the stew and simmer for 5 more minutes. Serve immediately.

St. Elmo Brewing Co.
In a city that appreciates artistic creativity and a good time, St. Elmo Brewing Co. fits right in. For the last several years, the brewery team has been welcoming neighbors and visitors into their ample taproom and beer garden for pints of Kölsch, lager, and whatever else has struck their fancy on brew day. Given St. Elmo's proximity to the airport, those in the know make it the first and last stop when spending a few days in Austin.

MAPLE SWEET-AND-SOUR MEATBALLS

Serves 12

MEATBALLS

1 Tbsp grapeseed oil
1 small yellow onion, chopped
1 red bell pepper, chopped
10 garlic cloves
1 tsp fine sea salt
⅓ cup whole milk
2 large eggs
3 cups panko breadcrumbs
1 Tbsp garlic powder
1 Tbsp onion powder
1 Tbsp chili powder
½ bunch fresh flat-leaf parsley
1 lb ground beef
1 lb ground pork
½ lb smoky bacon, minced

SAUCE

3 cups apple cider vinegar
2 cups apple cider
2 cups dark brown sugar
1½ cups your favorite sticky/
   sweet-style barbecue
   sauce
½ cup maple syrup
¼ cup your favorite hot sauce
¼ cup cornstarch

Switchback Brewing Co.

BURLINGTON, VERMONT

The Pairing: Rauchbier

A fun take on a party classic, this meatball recipe comes from Chef Dan Miele of Burlington's Bluebird Barbecue. The addition of smoky bacon goes well with a Rauchbier, which achieves its smoky flavor from smoked malts. Try a smoked lager like the Gates of Helles from the brewery. The sticky maple-based sweet-and-sour sauce, spiked with just a touch of heat and spice, calls for that next sip. Miele says this oven method turns out a delicious meatball, but if you have a smoker at home, he recommends smoking the meatballs over any fruitwood at 250°F for 15 minutes.

To make the meatballs: Preheat oven to 400°F. Line a baking sheet with foil or parchment paper.

In a large skillet, heat the grapeseed oil over medium heat. Add the onion, bell pepper, and garlic and a pinch of salt. Cook, stirring occasionally, for about 10 minutes, or until the onions are golden. Transfer to a blender and add the milk, eggs, breadcrumbs, garlic powder, onion powder, chili powder, and the remaining salt. Set aside 2 sprigs of parsley for garnish and add the rest to the blender. Blend until smooth then allow the mixture to cool.

In a large bowl, combine the ground beef, ground pork, bacon, and the blended vegetable mixture and mix well. Form the mixture into 1 in diameter rounds and arrange on the prepared baking sheet. Bake for 8 minutes, or until firm and beginning to brown.

To make the sauce: In a large saucepan, bring the vinegar, apple cider, brown sugar, barbecue sauce, maple syrup, and hot sauce to a simmer over medium heat, stirring occasionally.

In a small bowl, whisk the cornstarch with just enough water to dissolve it and make a slurry. Add the slurry to the sauce, turn the heat to high, and bring to a boil. Turn the heat to low, add the meatballs, cover, and cook, stirring occasionally, for 20 minutes, or until cooked through. Transfer the meatballs and sauce to serving dish. Chop the reserved parsley, sprinkle over the meatballs, and serve.

Switchback Brewing Co.

In a state where residents appreciate good beer and locally made products, every beer drinker has their personal favorite Switchback style. The cans and bottles might say "lager" or "IPA," but this brewery does things its own way, and someone looking for a boring, familiar pint won't find it here. From its Rauchbiers to its hoppy ales, Switchback's beers are well crafted and uniquely designed.

CRAB TORTELLINI WITH ROAST CHARD

Serves 6 to 8

TORTELLINI
2 cups all-purpose flour
2 large egg yolks

FILLING
1 Tbsp vegetable oil
½ white onion, finely diced
2 celery stalks, finely diced
1½ cups lump crabmeat
1 bunch fresh flat-leaf parsley,
    finely chopped
¾ cup ricotta cheese
¼ cup freshly grated
    Parmesan cheese
¼ cup heavy cream
1 large egg yolk
Zest of 1 lemon
1 heaping Tbsp Old Bay
    seasoning

continues ↗

Guinness Open Gate Brewery

HALETHORPE, MARYLAND

The Pairing: Blonde Ale

When the famed Irish brewery opened an expansive facility in Maryland, they embraced the local culture, including its food. This is a recipe for crab lovers who also enjoy a kick. Bomba Calabrese, or Italian bomba, is a spicy hot pepper spread that can be found in specialty shops, at grocery stores including Trader Joe's, or online, but feel free to substitute another chili spread. Pair with a blonde ale that complements the crab while also subduing some of the heat and spice.

To make the tortellini: In a food processor, combine flour, egg yolks, and ¼ cup water and process until uniform. (Alternatively, use a large bowl and knead by hand until smooth and elastic.) Tightly wrap the dough in plastic wrap and let rest at room temperature for 30 minutes.

Using a pasta machine, roll the dough out to the second thinnest setting. Cut the pasta sheets into 4 in diameter circles. Cover with damp paper towels and let stand at room temperature.

To make the filling: In a large sauté pan, heat the vegetable oil over low heat. Add the onion and celery and cook, stirring occasionally, for about 6 minutes, or until translucent. Transfer to a bowl and refrigerate until cold, about 1 hour.

Add the crabmeat, parsley, ricotta, Parmesan cheese, heavy cream, egg yolk, lemon zest, and Old Bay seasoning to the chilled onion mixture, gently combining by hand until well mixed and being careful to keep the crabmeat whole. Transfer to a piping bag with a large tip. Alternatively, fill a plastic food storage bag and cut a corner to push out the mixture.

Guinness Open Gate Brewery
For those with a hankering for a proper stout but not willing to fly to Dublin, Guinness made life easier by opening an impressive facility just outside of Baltimore. While the iconic stout is still made in Ireland, this brewery is creating a wonderful array of other styles, all under the expert hands that have defined Guinness quality since the 1700s.

1 Tbsp vegetable oil

2 celery stalks, diced

1 small sweet onion, diced

1 fennel bulb, diced

2 garlic cloves, minced

½ to ¾ cup bomba Calabrese

½ cup sherry

1½ cups blonde ale

2 qt crab stock

2 cups canned crushed
    tomatoes, puréed

2 bay leaves

Juice of 1 lemon

Old Bay seasoning (optional)

CHARD

1 bunch rainbow chard,
    stemmed and leaves
    chopped into ½ in pieces

2 Tbsp olive oil

Fine sea salt and freshly
    ground black pepper

FOR SERVING

1½ cups lump or jumbo lump
    crabmeat

Chopped fresh flat-leaf parsley

1 loaf sourdough bread, sliced
    and toasted

Brush each pasta disk lightly with water. Pipe about 1 Tbsp of crab filling into the center of each disk. Fold the disk in half over the filling to make a half circle. Press tightly with your fingers to make sure the edges are sealed. Bring the corners of the half circle together and pinch tightly to form a tortellini shape. Refrigerator for 1 hour to firm up the filling.

To make the stock: In a small stockpot, heat the vegetable oil over medium heat. Add the celery, onion, and fennel and cook, stirring occasionally, for 6 minutes, or until translucent. Add the garlic and cook, stirring, for 30 seconds, or until fragrant. Add the bomba Calabrese and cook, stirring, for 30 seconds. Add the sherry and simmer for about 5 minutes, or until almost evaporated. Add the beer and simmer for about 10 minutes, or until reduced by half. Add the crab stock, puréed tomatoes, and bay leaves and simmer for 45 minutes. Season with lemon juice, salt, and Old Bay seasoning (if using). Keep hot.

To make the chard: Preheat the oven to 400°F.

On a baking sheet, toss the chard with the olive oil and season with salt and pepper. Spread the chard in a single even layer and roast for about 10 minutes, or until starting to crisp on the edges—the leaves may start to brown or char a bit.

To serve: Use the roasted chard to line the bottom of a serving bowl.

Bring a large pot of heavily salted water to a rolling boil. Drop the tortellini into the boiling water and boil for 4 minutes, or until cooked through.

Meanwhile, add the crabmeat to the hot stock and cook for 3 minutes.

Using a slotted spoon, gently lift the tortellini out of water and arrange on top of the chard bowl, sitting the tortellini on their bottoms.

Use a ladle to scoop about 1 cup of stock over the pasta. Sprinkle with parsley and serve with toasted sourdough bread.

BEER TEMPURA WITH PALE-ALE DIPPING SAUCE

Serves 2 to 4

DIPPING SAUCE
1½ cups American pale ale
1 tsp freshly grated ginger
1 garlic clove, minced
½ cup Sriracha
¼ cup light brown sugar
1 tsp honey
1 tsp soy sauce

TEMPURA
¾ cup American pale ale, chilled
1 cup chickpea flour
1 Tbsp garlic powder
1 tsp paprika
2 large egg whites
Vegetable oil, for frying

—

Suggested tempura ingredients:
- 1 lb peeled shrimp
- 1 lb boneless, skinless chicken breast, cut into 1 in pieces
- asparagus, cut into ½ in pieces

Community Beer Works
BUFFALO, NEW YORK

The Pairing: Cream Ale

This very simple batter is big on flavor and can add a light and crispy element to any of your favorite foods, from seafood to meats, vegetables, or anything else you want to fry up. Because this is a quick-fry recipe, make sure any proteins or vegetables are cooked thoroughly before battering and frying. Pair with a cream ale that is crisp and slightly fruity. The sweetness of the beer will balance the savory nature of the dish and will not weigh down your palate.

To make the dipping sauce: In a small saucepan, bring the beer, ginger, and garlic to a boil. Continue boiling for 6 to 10 minutes, or until reduced by half. Add the Sriracha, brown sugar, honey, and soy sauce and boil for 5 more minutes. Remove from the heat and allow to cool slightly.

To make the tempura: Put the beer in the freezer for 10 minutes to ensure it's very cold.

In a medium bowl, combine the chickpea flour, garlic powder, and paprika. Sift together twice to ensure all clumps are gone.

In a large bowl, whip the egg whites until frothy then add the very cold beer and whip until combined. Slowly whisk the beer and egg white mixture into the chickpea flour mixture.

Fill a large Dutch oven or deep skillet with about 1 in of vegetable oil and heat to 375°F on a thermometer. Line a baking sheet with paper towels. Working in batches, dip the cooked meats, seafood, or vegetables into the batter, shaking off any excess, then carefully add to the hot oil and fry for 2 minutes, or until the tempura is golden brown. Transfer to the paper towel–lined baking sheet to drain. Dip and fry the remaining meat, seafood, or vegetables, adjusting the heat as needed to keep the oil at 375°F.

Serve the tempura hot with the dipping sauce.

Community Beer Works

For this brewery in Buffalo, New York, the word "community"
isn't just a name—it's a guiding principle. The brewery has worked
tirelessly to serve its neighbors, help local organizations thrive, and
generally lead the way, through beer, in being good citizens of the
world. Occasionally, playful and style-bending beers come out of the
brewhouse, but they are known for making reliable and flavorful true-
to-style lagers and ales.

PEANUT BUTTER BONBONS

Serves 10

3 Tbsp unsalted butter,
  at room temperature
2 oz cream cheese, at room
  temperature
1 cup creamy peanut butter
1½ cups confectioners' sugar,
  plus more for dusting
¼ cup heavy cream
2 cups panko breadcrumbs
2 large eggs
3 cups canola oil
1 cup blueberries
¼ cup maple syrup

Sketchbook Brewing Co.

EVANSTON & SKOKIE, ILLINOIS

The Pairing: Scotch ale

These decadent little bites from Chef John Chiakulas of the L. Woods Tap & Pine Lodge in Lincolnwood, Illinois, are delicious to share after a robust beer dinner. Creamy, sweet, and a little savory, with a smack of tartness, they pair perfectly with a Scotch ale, such as the brewery's Lapwing. Sometimes called a wee heavy, Scotch ales are boozy and caramel-forward and often feature a slight peaty smoke note in the background. These bonbons are labor intensive, sure, but worth the work.

In a large bowl, beat together 2 Tbsp of the butter and the cream cheese until smooth. Add the peanut butter and mix to combine then gradually add the confectioners' sugar and mix until fully incorporated. Cover and refrigerate for about 1 hour, or until chilled. Add the heavy cream and mix until fully incorporated.

Put the breadcrumbs in a small bowl.

Using a tablespoon or small scoop, form the peanut butter mixture into small balls then drop the balls in the breadcrumbs, tossing and pressing to coat. Transfer the bonbons to a plate and refrigerate for 30 minutes. Reserve the breadcrumbs.

In a small bowl, whisk the eggs with 1 tsp of water.

Remove the bonbons from the refrigerator and dip each one in egg wash, followed by a second layer of breadcrumbs. Refrigerate for 10 minutes.

Fill a large Dutch oven, deep pot, or deep fryer with about 1 in of canola oil and heat to 350°F on a thermometer. Line a plate with paper towels. Working in batches, carefully add the bonbons to the hot oil and fry for 30 to 45 seconds, or until golden. Using a slotted spoon, transfer the bonbons to the paper towel–lined plate to drain. Repeat to fry the remaining bonbons, adjusting the heat as needed to keep the oil at 350°F. Keep warm.

In a small saucepan, combine the blueberries, maple syrup, and remaining 1 Tbsp of butter over medium heat. Cook, breaking up the berries while stirring, for about 10 minutes, or until the ingredients are well combined and a thin syrup forms.

Spoon some sauce onto small plates and top with warm bonbons. Dust with confectioners' sugar and serve.

Sketchbook Brewing Co.

Evanston, Illinois, has come a long way since its role in promoting Prohibition. That it hosts breweries today is a testament to progress, and chief among the city's breweries is Sketchbook. Founded by Cesar Marron, a home brewer who won the national Sam Adams Longshot competition years earlier, Sketchbook makes both regular and specialty batches, with an eye toward innovation and the future.

Group Pairings

Over the last twenty or so years, events have popped up around the United States where visitors can taste beer and cheese alongside each other. Other festivals feature coffee and beer, or doughnuts and beer. Annual events that celebrate bacon and beer are, of course, very popular. Wine versus beer dinners, where diners are encouraged to see which better complements the food, as well as how the beverages interact on the palate, are also increasingly common.

In this chapter, I encourage you to experience some fun and perhaps unusual beer pairings that you can try at home. Invite some friends over and make a day (or night) of it. I've included notes about which beers to pair with various other ingredients like doughnuts, cheese, chocolate, and even, wine.

Beer is versatile and can bring out the best in food, and vice versa. When it comes to pairings, it is not enough to simply think about the aromas and flavors of the beer—although that is a good place to start—but also the acidity, the fat, the mouthfeel, the alcohol warmth, and the salinity.

In the same way there are experts in beer, the same is true for nearly every food and drink category, with people diving into the nuances, flavors, and palate effects of all kinds of artisan foods and beverages.

These experts have discovered that beer is an ideal pairing companion, thanks to its vast array of styles. The flavors and aromas present in beer bring nuance to food items, elevating the tastes to new heights. Carbonation and mouthfeel also contribute to pairing success. There is endless potential for pairing thanks to the diversity of beer.

While festivals and themed dinners are fun, they are often chaotic, busy, and rushed. They're great for a night out and a shared experience, but also curated to the tastes of a place or chef. Creating a pairing at home offers a different experience. You can go at your own pace and focus on parings that intrigue you, or are novel to you, or that are just comfortable and familiar. You can eat and drink as much or as little as you like.

Themed beer pairings are a great way to bring friends together as well. Foods and flavors can spark memories and foster conversation, bringing nourishment aside from just caloric content to our bodies.

The experts on the following pages have dedicated good portions of their lives to the pursuit of the flavors, processes, and history of their respective fields. They've also all enjoyed tipping back a pint of beer now and again.

Start with these pairing suggestions and grow your own tastings from there. There is fun and satisfaction in having a table filled with cheese or chocolate with glasses of beer strewn about, tasting and sampling to find a truly joyful connection.

DOUGHNUTS

America's love affair with doughnuts is relatively new, and it took the "craft" segment to turn it into a modern object of devotion, says Brian Yaeger, an author, journalist, and founder of Baker's Dozen, a beer and doughnut pairing event that takes place annually in Portland, Oregon. The same can be said for doughnuts.

"I think that doughnuts, by virtue of being as old a part of the American fabric as beer, were overlooked," explains Yaeger, who is a proponent of the traditional spelling of the breakfast staple, versus the more modern "donut."

Doughnuts, like beer, are going through a renaissance, and a new generation of bakers are bringing exciting flavors and techniques to the snack, while still honoring tradition, much in the same way brewers are treating beer. It makes sense, says Yaeger, since the two overlap in many ways. Both are made of grain, both balance sweetness and texture, and both offer endless opportunity for creativity.

"When you combine beer and doughnuts in a thoughtful way, they really are greater than the sum of their parts and head into new and fun directions," adds Yaeger.

To help start a day off right, here are a dozen beer and doughnut pairing suggestions from Yaeger, with styles and flavors that are easily found at most shops.

Apple Fritter and Old Ale
A big, boozy beer pairs well with bulkier doughnuts. Old ale is rich with raisin and intricate spice notes that suit the heaviness of the apples in the fritters. This is a pairing that embraces gluttony.

Buttermilk Bar and Cream Ale
The lightness of cream ale and its touch of sweetness let this old-fashioned rectangular doughnut do the heavy lifting, and it does the job beautifully, thanks to its dense texture and sugary glaze. This is a palate cleanser pairing.

Raspberry Jelly Doughnut and Vanilla Porter
This is not a pairing to overthink. There is a lot of harmony that comes with combining the chocolate, coffee, and vanilla flavors of the beer and the sweet, slightly tart preserved fruit in the doughnut. It's an unctuous pairing that is sure to please.

Lemon Jelly Doughnut and an American Hefeweizen
Hefeweizen is often served with a lemon garnish. Here, the doughnut acts as the fruit. Its tart, sweet, and light citrus bite enhances the wheat character of the beer.

Peanut Butter Pocket or Peanut Butter Glazed and a Bavarian Hefeweizen
A traditional hefeweizen has a banana aroma to it, and here, the peanut butter in or on the doughnut creates a combination akin to the famed Elvis sandwich. Banana, a little spice, and sweet nuttiness equals perfection.

Boston Cream Doughnut and Graham Cracker Porter
Think of this pairing as creating a s'more, with the cream of the doughnut taking the place of the marshmallow.

Maple Bacon Doughnut and Rauchbier
Here, the smoky bacon bits and sweet syrup of the doughnut accent similar flavors in the smoked malt beer, which calls to mind ham, bacon, and campfires.

Spice Cake Doughnut and Double IPA

With this pairing, the baking spices act as a foil to the bitterness of the hops in the IPA, while also complementing the generous malt bill.

Chocolate Glazed Devil's Food Cake Doughnut and Kriek

This pairing is reminiscent of Black Forest cake. The acidity of the cherry-fermented beer brings out additional sweetness in the chocolate.

Churro and Scotch Ale

The caramel malts in the ale add additional sweetness and round out the spiciness of the churro. This internationally inspired pairing is decadent.

Glazed Doughnut and Schwarzbier

The most popular doughnut pairs wonderfully with a dark lager. This lighter, sweeter doughnut gets a touch of coffee and roast from the beer without adding any additional sugar to the palate.

Cake Doughnut and Coffee Stout

While most doughnuts are fried in batches, cake doughnuts are sometimes fried to order at establishments in the know. They are also made with baking powder or baking soda, as opposed to yeast, giving them a thicker texture. When served warm, a coffee stout, rich in java flavors and aromas, makes perfect sense.

COFFEE

Coffee and beer are like beverage bookends. One is typically consumed in the morning and the other at night, but on certain days or occasions the two can be flipped. For longtime drinkers of stouts and porters, the taste of coffee is apparent in the brew, even if no beans were used. Thanks to roasted grains, the longer the kiln, the more likely a beer will take on notes of coffee.

At first blush, it might not seem the two have a lot in common flavorwise, but they share many taste similarities. Both beverages are also aroma driven, and each is a regular part of many people's daily lives. Coffee is regularly finding its way into beers, thanks in part to the ingenuity of today's brewers, their relationship with local roasters, and increasing customer demand.

Porters and stouts, beers that already have coffee flavors because of the malts used in the brewing process, are often dosed with additional cold-brew coffee during the fermentation process or blended with cold brew afterward to create a richer java experience without the additional acidity that could come from steeping beans in hot water.

When beer comes together, the combined flavors of water, malt, hops, and yeast impart a wide swath of flavors that mimic many familiar tastes and aromas. In coffee, the flavors of just the beans range from floral and fruity (blueberry, lemon, peach, apricot, and more) to nutty and smoky.

When thinking about creating a home pairing experience, like a cupping or beer tasting, find flavors that can work together: a witbier or hefeweizen with a lemony coffee, a bready and sweet cream ale or a Helles lager with a coffee boasting blueberry notes. A Costa Rican coffee with sweet sugar notes, stone fruit aromas, and citrus can be paired with an American pale ale, a hazy IPA, or even a Scotch ale. Ethiopian coffee can be floral with herbal and fruity notes and pairs nicely with farmhouse ales. Sweet Sumatran coffee can find companions in brown ales or Schwarzbiers, as well as a Belgian-style dubbel.

As your beer-pairing journey continues, look for the flavor descriptors on different coffee

beans and let your mind wander to beer flavors and aromas and then brew up some cups and pour some pints to see if they work together. Also, smelling beans before and after grinding might reveal aromas that will steer you in the direction of potential beer pairings. Inhaling aromas after the coffee has been properly brewed might introduce new flavors to the mix as well. Trust your palate and your instincts.

Just as beer should be served at cellar temperature or slightly below, depending on the style, when consuming hot coffee, temperature is important. Coffee is best consumed at 95°F to 130°F because the flavors are more articulate at those levels. And in the same way that proper glassware is key for beer, so too is the case with coffee. Look for a mug or cup with a wide opening to allow aromas to escape from the liquid. Pint glasses should be avoided for beer, and the same is true with paper cups for coffee.

If a side-by-side tasting is not in the cards, sampling a coffee beer (to go along with some doughnuts, perhaps? see page 203) has never been easier. Along with the coffee-added stouts and porters, and barrel-aged versions, brewers are putting coffee in everything from IPAs to cream ales to bitters and beyond.

CHEESE

There is a natural friendship between beer and cheese. Wine comes up time and time again as a wonderful pairing, but honestly, beer has more in common with dairy. Consider, as others have said before, that cows and goats eat grass and grain and then produce milk, which is turned into cheese. Grain is used in the production of beer. Maybe it happens, but few, if any, have seen Bessie eat a bunch of grapes.

There has been a revolution in artisan cheese making, following a few bland decades where mass-produced, flavorless yellow blocks ruled the dairy aisle. Beer followed a similar story. In the few decades following Prohibition until its resurgence in the 1980s, the majority of beer made in the United States was bland, light lager. Now choice is available for both beer and cheese like never before.

Adding hops, flavorful yeasts, robust grains, fruit, herbs, and more to beer creates endless opportunities for cheese pairings, but carbonation is also a benefit. The scrubbing effect of carbonation on the tongue helps keep the palate sharp against fatty or dense cheese.

Finding pairings that work is not overly difficult. Countless cheeses being made around the world incorporate local flora and flavors, so in many cases, you can simply look for where a cheese was made and find beer styles native to that area. Chances are, they will share some similarities that bring new flavors to the forefront. Alternatively, visit your local cheese shop (the really good ones also have a beer section), pick out a few of each, get a table, and get to pouring.

Or take the advice of John David Ryan. He is the current brand ambassador at Aslan Brewing Company in Bellingham, Washington, but cut his teeth on beer and cheese pairings at Murray's Cheese in Manhattan, one of the country's top spots for specialty fromage.

Ryan shares a few of his favorite and most inspired pairings below. When doing a tasting at home, he likes to build flavor, keeping it simple at first and then getting more ambitious. He calls this approach "mild to wild."

Mozzarella or Burrata and Kriek
There is a reason people pair this cheese with tomato: the acidity. Krieks offer up a similar effect, especially light-bodied krieks with tart, fruity acidity and a touch of sourness. A simple cheese does not need a simple beer.

Fresh Goat Cheese or Chèvre and Saison

Fresh goat cheese has a lot of earthiness and is fluffy and creamy. A fresh and funky saison, with its straw and grass notes and tangy brightness with lemony or orange notes, really makes for a beautiful pairing.

Brie and Pilsner

There is a delicious buttery character to Brie, which also has a broccoli, mushroom, and cauliflower essence that is complemented by a crisp and clean pilsner. A well-carbonated one cleans the palate between bites.

Taleggio and Witbier

I love a fresh-washed-rind cheese because it is often simple with some depth. A beer that is bright and lemony with a touch of sweetness, like a witbier, really lets the cheese do its thing and unfold.

Cheddar and India Pale Ale

An assertive Cheddar cheese gets a boost from a traditional hoppy West Coast IPA that has a prominent smooth malt character and earthy yet citrus-forward hops.

Comté and Brown Ale

A classic American brown ale, with some nutty flavors and a touch of sweetness, complements the nutty sweetness of the cheese. Anything too hoppy or bitter would just overwhelm it.

Manchego and Festbier or Oktoberfest

A crisp but slightly sweet and nutty lager stands up to this rich, slightly fatty, and salty cheese.

Aged Gouda and Pumpkin Ale

A sweet butterscotch note from the cheese gets a boost from the traditional pie spices that go into the beer.

Blue Cheese and Barrel-Aged Coconut Stout

Everyone has a different opinion on blue cheese, but I like the sweet and tangy approach (in a blue). A rich, thick, boozy stout, plus the oak character from the barrel, stands up to the body of the cheese. A little bit of coconut brings sweetness into the mix.

Spicy Cheese and Rauchbier

If you come across jalapeño cream cheese or rich goat cheese with spicy pepper, Rauchbier works well. The smoke brings out more of the pepper heat, while the bacon aromas of the beer are smoothed by the silkiness of the cheese.

CHOCOLATE

———

Pete Slosberg takes chocolate seriously. He wants you to do the same. The cofounder of Pete's Brewing Company (of Pete's Wicked Ale fame), one of the early popular craft beer brands, and later the chocolate label Cocoa Pete's Chocolate Adventures, he has spent a lot of time seeking "magical" pairings between beer and chocolate and says it is a lofty goal that is often hard to achieve.

That doesn't mean we shouldn't try.

"Beer and chocolate can be so similar," says Slosberg. "They are complementary and contrasting, and pairings can range from off-the-wall bad to incredible." He thinks about both beer and chocolate as bitter and sweet and tries to find pairings that work in those arenas. Pure chocolate starts off as very bitter and is then sweetened with milk or sugar. Many commercially available chocolates are sweetened with additional sugar, artificial flavors, and vegetable oils.

In finding pairings that work, nuance is important. So is freshness. Slosberg is a proponent of freshly tapped beer, as close to its release date as

possible, so it tastes the way the brewer intended. Beer that's been sitting in a cooler or on a shelf for months and starting to fade will do no favors to the chocolate, he says.

The same is true for the chocolate itself. There are artisan chocolate makers who take great care with their ingredients. The three main kinds of chocolate are dark, milk, and white. Dark chocolate, says Slosberg, can have fruity, sour, spicy, and brownie notes. Milk chocolate imparts caramel, milky, and sour flavors. White chocolate can be buttery and vanilla-like.

As with other beer pairings, Slosberg says there are no hard and fast rules. The stars must align for a magical beer and chocolate pairing, but there are some guidelines that work. Start with pairings that progress from sweet to bitter. Avoid pairing bitter beers with bitter chocolate; it just doesn't work. Malted milk balls often pair well with a traditional IPA, where the sweetness of the grain is accented by the confection, which in return enhances the citrusy aspects of the hops. Milk chocolate and pilsners often pair well together, with the chocolate's milky and caramel attributes standing up to the crisp body and earthy hops in the beer. Belgian dark ales that are already peppery and fruity, like Chimay Blue, get a boost from cherry-infused chocolates.

How you eat the chocolate is also important, Slosberg says. It is not simply enough to take a bite and then a swallow of beer. That process does not allow the chocolate to fully reveal itself. It is best, he says, to take a small bite of chocolate and let it melt fully on your tongue, coating it and allowing the chocolate's full flavors to envelop your palate. Then take a whiff of the beer to introduce its aromas, and then a small sip to let the flavors mingle with the chocolate, creating new and hopefully exciting combinations.

While it may be tempting to pair flavors that are already in the chocolate, the real fun comes with seeking out complementary or contrasting flavors to bring out the nuances of both. There is no shortage of chocolate beers on the market (and don't forget the pastry stouts, which are usually big and boozy and made to resemble desserts), and any of them would be an easy layup. But for fun, try to find beers that don't feature cocoa in a prominent way when choosing a pairing.

Here are a few pairings that I have enjoyed in the past and will bring some pop to your next gathering.

Coconut Cream and Lime-Accented Gose
The beer will highlight the tropical coconut flavor and create the experience of a piña colada, if only for a minute, like a mini island vacation.

Chocolate-Covered Almonds and Brown Ale
A simple pub ale with soft flavors of chocolate, coffee, and toffee will serve the dark chocolate–covered nuts well, creating a vanilla and marzipan-like flavor.

Chocolate-Covered Peanuts and Irish Stout
One bar staple deserves another. Here the dark chocolate covering the peanuts gets a boost from the coffee and chocolate notes of the ale. The creamy mouthfeel from the nitro pour is a nice contrast to the crunchiness of the legume.

Raspberry Cream and Barrel-Aged Belgian-Style Tripel
Paired together, the result is an oaky, vanilla, nutty, effervescent ale that is well served and complemented by the smooth, fresh, candied-raspberry flavor of the chocolate.

Toffee and English Bitter
The subtleness of bitters—they're not really as bitter as the name would suggest—with caramel, a light red fruitiness, and just a touch of sweetness,

makes excellent background music for the candy in the spotlight. Toffee, a brittle candy with brown sugar and butterscotch flavors, gets a lift from the roundness of the beer. Two fine English traditions, together at last.

Chocolate Truffle and Jalapeño Pale Ale

A little heat and a little citrus in the beer is a fun complement to the sweet earthiness of chocolate truffles. There are a lot of hot-pepper beers on the market today, and while you likely want one where the capsaicin isn't too assertive, just a little spice is a fun exercise for the palate, especially during dessert.

Caramel and Schwarzbier

The classic dessert plays into the depth of both the baked sugar and light roast in the beer. The Schwarzbier's effervescence brings a lightness to the overall duo.

Almond Nougat and Honey Ale

Honey has been showing up more and more in beers, and its sweet and sticky character is accented when paired with almond nougat. In many cases, honey in a beer adds depth to the body of the ale or lager and is a nice pairing to this already dense candy, for a feeling of decadence all around.

WINE

There's an old saying that it takes a lot of great beer to make a great wine—the idea being that the vintners and field workers enjoy a cold glass of beer after a long, hot day in the sun tending to the grapes before they turn into vino.

Even with that sentiment, over the decades, a rivalry has emerged between beer and wine, promoting the idea that they are enemies that need to be pitted against each other. The opposite is true, of course. Drinkers can prefer one over the other, but there is a lot of crossover appeal.

At home, at restaurants, and at bars, beer and wine (and spirits too) share the same space and do so largely in harmony. Still, there are books where authors like to compare styles of wine to styles of beer. There are dinners hosted where guests are given pours of each with a course and asked to choose which is better. (Of course, beer pairs better with food than wine does, but that is not the point here.)

There is a natural kinship in these fermented beverages, and while the ingredients are different, the enjoyment of drinking beer alongside wine is something that should be experienced. Someone does not need to be exclusively a "wine person" or a "beer person," but often they feel siloed. There is also a whole new set of lessons and flavor profiles to learn, and so people often stick to what they know. I encourage cross drinking.

Lauren Buzzeo, the managing editor of *Wine Enthusiast* magazine, knows a lot about finding the right connection between wine and beer and offers up these suggestions for teasing out how the attributes of specific beer styles compare to those of different wines.

This guide may also help bring the wine-minded into the beer space.

With its typically pronounced characteristics of bright citrus and green apple, as well as a good dose of sea-spray minerality, if **Spanish Albariño** is your vinous go-to, consider swapping in a Gose. The traditional German-style sour wheat beer not only offers a similarly vibrant flavor profile but is also often brewed with coriander and sea salt, yielding a welcome and familiar saline kick to the experience.

If a classic **Cabernet Sauvignon**—with its structured tannins, pronounced oak, and rich, ripe plum and berry fruits throughout—is your wine jam, consider a barrel-aged stout for your beer-drinking pleasure. While the beer might not carry the same fruity intensity as a California Cab, it will offer a familiar bold profile from start to finish, with ample toasty, roasty notes on the palate and a long, lingering finish that won't easily relent.

Argentine Malbec is known for being generally upfront in ripe fruit aromas and flavors, as well as moderate in structure, with framing tannins and a lingering finish. A similarly upfront and not-shy Belgian-style dark ale will provide a comparable experience, thanks to a pleasant interplay between ripe fruit and rich, slightly roasted malt flavors that results in a similarly smooth and creamy experience from start to finish. With a general decadence that's hard to ignore or dislike, a sweet stout will prove an easy swap for fans of that experience, just with a little less overt fruitiness.

Fans of **Nebbiolo**, the grape used to make Barolo and Barbaresco, among other wines, may find a familiar nuance and complexity of flavor in a Belgian-style Oud Bruin. Similarities can be found between the two, thanks to the beer style's long aging process and layers that range from vibrant acidity to plum and cherry fruits, accents of caramel-like richness, and hits of wood spice throughout—all things one would look for in a quality Nebbiolo-based pour.

Known for its expressive fruit-forward profiles and affinity for pairing with spicy fare, **Riesling** is a foodie darling of the wine world. A suitable sudsy sub would be a juicy or hazy IPA dominated by fruity hop characteristics over those that present earthy, piney, or resiny ones. Options made with hop varieties like Citra, Galaxy, or Mosaic will do the trick nicely.

Depending on whether you prefer cool- or warm-climate **Sauvignon Blanc**, consider a traditional American IPA to fit your beer bill. Bottlings made with New Zealand's Sauvin hop can express similar tones to a cool-climate Sauvy, like gooseberry, tart plum, white grape, and a touch of pepperiness, while those who prefer warm-climate Sauvignon Blanc can opt for more ripe stone-fruit-forward IPAs like those brewed with Mosaic or El Dorado hops.

And finally, **natural wine**. Regardless of the grape any given product is made from, if you're into the natty wine scene, you're likely going to love sour beers, with their similarly funky and vibrantly mouth-puckering profiles. Since American wild ales carry a range of stylistic interpretations and flavor and aroma characteristics, start traditional with lambics like gueuze for high natural impact and go forth to other deliciously soured selections from there.

ACKNOWLEDGMENTS

Writing a book can be a lonely experience, even when writing about a social beverage and the experience of gathering for a meal. Add in a pandemic where in-person research and meetings are replaced by video chats and phone calls, and the process perpetually feels like a table for one.

Thankfully, when I get to leave the home office, I walk into a house with my wonderful wife, April, my daughter, Hannah, and our loyal mutt, Pepper. The days and adventures I get to spend with them are always my happiest. Their support and love is invaluable. Our meals together are always the best.

The same is true with my parents, John and Carolyn; my mother-in-law, Teresa; and my siblings, Amanda, Todd, Bill, Valerie, Dan, Thomas, Marie, Jill, and Becket. Plus the ever-growing cadre of nieces and nephews. Family makes meals taste better.

Drinks with friends are awesome. Even though most have been virtual or distanced during the writing of this book, the pints and conversations with friends, including Jason Gareis, Mike Alfonzo, Michael Napolitano, Jeff Alworth, Lew Bryson, Em Sauter, Don Tse, Chris Shepard, Chris Sidwa, Stan Hieronymus, Maureen Ogle, Jeff Cioletti, Ben Keene, Brian Yaeger, Josh Noel, Carla Lauter, Mike Storer, Josh Tomson, Cheoma Smith, and Nate Schweber.

Every week, I show up at work and write words and record podcasts. My colleagues and friends at *Beer Edge*, Andy Crouch and Liz Melby, make it fun every day. I'm also grateful to Brad Ring, Kiev Rattee, and Dawson Raspuzzi at *BYO* magazine.

I'm indebted to Lauren Buzzeo, who offered me the gig of a lifetime, reviewing beers and writing articles for *Wine Enthusiast* magazine. My opportunity to write about a dynamic and complicated industry has made for an exciting career and ultimately led to this book.

Because I'm a guy with a lot of jobs, once a week I spend a few hours with Augie Carton, Justin Kennedy, and Brian Casse. We've been hosting the *Steal This Beer* podcast for seven years now, and along the way what I've learned about food, wine, dining, and just celebrating life from these gentlemen, as well as our countless guests, has helped inform and shape my writing.

My deepest thanks to everyone at Princeton Architectural Press, led by Lynn Grady, for the trust in bringing this book to life and the passion behind the editing, marketing, and sales effort. Holly La Due joined the project late in the process, but with a great eye and true professionalism focused the pages and guided the book to its final form. I'm thankful for that. Sara Stemen, Lauren Salkeld, and Monica Parcell sharpened the words and recipes, and the design team of Paul Wagner and Natalie Snodgrass made each page pop with color and crispness.

Jenny Stephens has guided me through several projects, including this one, and has been a constant champion, voice of reason, and steadying force during sometimes difficult days. She's the best.

I spent five very happy years working with Jon Page when we ran *All About Beer* magazine and having the chance to do it again on this book is a real gift. His good humor, hard work, critical eye, and zest for life inspire me.

To the brewers, chefs, and brewery professionals who contributed recipes, spent time being interviewed, and shared tips and insight, I simply cannot thank you enough. This book is a collection of your knowledge, and I'm grateful for your trust. First rounds (and the following) are on me.

The hospitality industry is critically important to society, and while workers in the space are often taking the brunt of bad customer attitudes, a word of thanks to the brewers, chefs, kitchen staff, bartenders, and front-of-house teams that keep the world moving. Life is better because of what you do and create.

—*JOHN HOLL*

To my entire family, thanks for your support and enthusiasm throughout this project. To my amazing wife, Carie, thanks for your eternal optimism and for always encouraging me to take giant leaps. Growing a bountiful herb garden just in time for shooting this cookbook was icing on the cake. To Lincoln and Eliza, thanks for taste testing many of these meals, and I look forward to drinking beers with you in a couple of decades.

When I was staring up a mountain of a deadline, my sisters helped guide me to the summit. Thanks to Beth Glueck for making the long drive for a marathon weekend of cooking. And tremendous thanks to the saintly Lauri Palko, who eagerly volunteered countless hours of planning, cooking, baking, and styling to make these photographs a reality. I am ever grateful for your assistance, and I cherish our new tradition of weekly family dinners. A hearty thanks to John Palko as well, for your assistance and wisecracking.

Cheers to the beer community in Asheville, North Carolina, for (safely) welcoming me to photograph your beers and breweries during a pandemic. Special thanks to Katie Smith, Kaitlin Trimboli, and Eeva Redmond of Highland Brewing; Shanda Crowe and Javier Bolea of Hi-Wire Brewing; Ashlee Mooneyhan, Scott Sowers, and Jessie Massie of Sierra Nevada Brewing Co.; and John Parks of Zillicoah Beer Co. I'm also grateful for the folks at Appalachian Vintner (especially Chris Whaley and Michael Schattschneider), who regularly helped me find the perfect beer style to pair with a recipe.

And to my great friend John Holl, thanks for inviting me on this journey. I'd follow you anywhere, especially if good beer is involved.

—*JON PAGE*

LIST OF BREWERIES

The breweries are listed in the order they appear in the book. Several recipes originated with the author or an individual chef and are not listed here.

Chapter One

Heirloom Rustic Ales
2113 E Admiral Blvd
Tulsa, OK 74110
(918) 292-8757
www.heirloomrusticales.com
Recipe by: Chris Castro
Tacos de Papa, Page 16

Chuckanut Brewery and Kitchen
11937 Higgins Airport Way
Burlington, WA 98233
(360) 752-3377
chuckanutbreweryandkitchen.com
Recipe by: Ben Fulks
A.B.L.T. Salad, Page 18

Jack's Abby Craft Lagers
100 Clinton St,
Framingham, MA 01702
(508) 872-0900
jacksabby.com
Recipe by: Mo Bentley
House Lager Mussels with Zhoug,
Page 21

Rockwell Beer Company
1320 S Vandeventer Ave
St. Louis, MO 63110
(314) 256-1657
www.rockwellbeer.com
Recipe by: Brian Moxey
Deviled Eggs, Page 22

Bierstadt Lagerhaus
2875 Blake St
Denver, CO 80205
(720) 570-7824
bierstadtlager.com
Recipe by: Ashleigh Carter
Breakfast Burrito with New Mexican
Red Chile Sauce, Page 24

Bow and Arrow Brewing Co.
608 McKnight Ave NW
Albuquerque, NM 87102
(505) 247-9800
www.bowandarrowbrewing.com
Recipe by: Lois Ellen Frank
Hominy Corn Posole, Page 26

Heater Allen Brewing
907 NE 10th Ave
McMinnville, OR 97128
(503) 472-4898
heaterallen.com
Recipe by: Lisa Allen
Mushroom and Root Vegetable
Biscuit Pot Pie, Page 28

Enegren Brewing Company
444 Zachary St #120
Moorpark, CA 93021
(805) 552-0602
www.enegrenbrewing.com
Recipe by: John Bird
Jägerschnitzel, Page 30

Wibby Brewing
209 Emery St
Longmont, CO 80501
(303) 776-4594
www.wibbybrewing.com
Recipe by: Ryan Wibby
Fish and Chips, Page 32

Hop Butcher for the World
Chicago, IL
www.hopbutcher.com
Recipe by: Todd Davies & Laurie
McNamara
Whipped Ricotta with Honey,
Thyme, and Toasted Ciabatta,
Page 35

Chapter Two

Springdale Beer Company
102 Clinton St
Framingham, MA 01702
(774) 777-5085
springdalebeer.com
Recipe by: Dave Punch
Spicy Fish Ceviche with Grilled
Pineapple, Page 41

Drekker Brewing Co.
1666 1st Ave N
Fargo, ND 58102
(701) 532-0506
drekkerbrewing.com
Recipe by: Ryan Nitschke and
Luna Fargo
Mushroom and Vegetable Dumplings
with Mango Chili Nuoc Cham,
Page 42

Weathered Souls Brewing
606 Embassy Oaks #500
San Antonio, TX 78216
(210) 274-6824
weatheredsouls.beer/
Recipe by: Andrew Samia
Spicy Brussels Sprouts, Page 45

Reuben's Brews
5010 14th Ave NW
Seattle, WA 98107
(206) 784-2859
reubensbrews.com
Recipe by: Robert Tague
Merguez Spiced Lamb Burger,
Page 46

SingleSpeed Brewing Company
325 Commercial St
Waterloo, IA 50701
(319) 883-3604
www.singlespeedbrewing.com
Recipes by: Kegan Bakken
Brined Pork Chops with Maple Glaze
and Apple Chutney, Page 48
Honey Glazed Carrots, Page 49
Spaetzle and Beerchamel Cheese
Sauce, Page 51

Hopewell Brewing Co.
2760 N Milwaukee Ave
Chicago, IL 60647
(773) 698-6178
www.hopewellbrewing.com
Recipe by: Palita Sriratana
Gaeng Hang Lae, Page 52

Bonn Place Brewing Co.
310-14 Taylor St
Bethlehem, PA 18015
(610) 419-6660
www.bonnbrewing.com
Recipe by Sam Masotto
The Adult Peanut Butter and Jelly
Sandwich, Page 55

Edmund's Oast Brewing Co.
1505 King St #115
Charleston, SC 29405
(843) 718-3224
edmundsoast.combrewing-co/
Recipe by: Heather Hutton
Citrus Tres Leches Cake with Orange
Blossom and Basil, Page 56

Chapter Three

**Eventide Oyster Co. /
Allagash Brewing Company**
50 Industrial Way
Portland, ME 04103
(207) 878-5385
www.allagash.com
Fresh Oysters with Mignonette and
Cocktail Sauce, Page 62

Wolf's Ridge Brewing
215 N 4th St
Columbus, OH 43215
(614) 429-3936
www.wolfsridgebrewing.com
Recipe by: Seth Lassak
"Steak and Eggs," Page 64

Primitive Beer
2025 Ionosphere St
Longmont, CO 80504
primitive.beer/
Recipe by: Anthony W. Lopiccolo
A Better Caesar Salad, Page 66

Fogtown Brewing Co.
25 Pine St
Ellsworth, ME 04605
(207) 370-0845
www.fogtownbrewing.com
Recipe by: Kat Courant
Roasted Mushroom and Garlic
Bisque with Pan Toasted Baguette,
Page 68

Coppertail Brewing
2601 E 2nd Ave
Tampa, FL 33605
(813) 247-1500
coppertailbrewing.com
Recipe by: Casey Hughes
Spicy Tapenade Ragu with Linguine,
Page 71

Aslan Brewing Co.
1330 N Forest St
Bellingham, WA 98225
(360) 393-4106
aslanbrewing.com
Recipe by: Adam Grossman
Grilled Tofu with Fruity Korean
Barbecue Sauce, Page 72

Alesong Brewing & Blending
80848 Territorial Hwy
Eugene, OR 97405
(541) 844-9925
www.alesongbrewing.com
Recipe by: Matt Van Wyk
Spice-Rubbed Pork Blade Steaks
with Barbecue Sauce, Page 74

Chapter Four

Good Word Brewing & Public House
3085 Main St
Duluth, GA 30096
(678) 336-9928
goodwordbrewing.com
Recipe by: Brian Crain
Warm Farro, Mushroom, and Romanesco Salad with Roasted Poblano Sauce, Page 84

Bissell Brothers
38 Resurgam Pl.
Portland, ME 04102
(207) 808-8258
bissellbrothers.com
Recipe by: MacGreagor Stevenson
Baked Beer Beans, Page 87

Roadhouse Pub & Eatery
20 E Broadway Ave
Jackson, WY 83001
(307) 739-0700
roadhousebrewery.com
Shrimp, Sausage, and Grits, Page 88

Atlas Brew Works
2052 West Virginia Ave NE #102
Washington, DC 20002
(202) 832-0420
www.atlasbrewworks.com
Recipe by: Daniel Vilarrubi
Long-Simmer Weekend Chili, Page 91

By All Means Brew Lab
1400 S 24th St W #3
Billings, MT 59102
(406) 534-3075
byallmeansbeer.com
Recipe by: Travis Zeilstra
Short Ribs Rellenos, Page 92

Blackberry Farm Brewery
106 Everett Ave
Maryville, TN 37804
blackberryfarmbrewery.com
Recipe by: Josh Feathers
Coffee- and Chili-Rubbed Venison Loin with Romesco Sauce, Page 94

Chapter Five

Fair State Brewing Cooperative
2506 Central Ave NE
Minneapolis, MN 55418
(612) 444-3209
fairstate.coop/
Recipe by: Kadi Kaelin
Chicken Liver Mousse with Red Onion Marmalade, Page 104

Sierra Nevada Brewing Co.
100 Sierra Nevada Way
Fletcher, NC 28732
(828) 708-6242
sierranevada.com
Recipe by: Jessie Massie
Spring Greens Salad with Lemon IPA Vinaigrette and Grilled Trout, Page 106

Gotahold Brewing
409 W Van Buren
Eureka Springs, AR 72632
(479) 363-4187
gotahold.beer/
Recipe by: Wendy Reese Hartmann
Lemony White Bean and Sausage Soup, Page 108

Lost Worlds Brewing
19700-D, One Norman Blvd.
Cornelius, NC 28031
(980) 689-2467
www.lostworldsbeer.com
Recipe by: Sasha Quinn
Shroomin' Philly with Agave Mustard, Page 111

Pacifica Brewery
4627 CA-1
Pacifica, CA 94044
(650) 735-5311
www.pacificabrewery.beer/
Recipe by: Sylvain Montassier
Croque Madame with Beer Pretzel Bread, Page 112

Wallenpaupack Brewing Co.
73 Welwood Ave
Hawley, PA 18428
(650) 735-5311
www.wallenpaupackbrewingco.com
Recipe by: Scott Jones and Eric Ives
Tempura-Battered Shrimp Tacos, Page 114

Chapter Six

New Realm Brewing Co.
550 Somerset Terrace NE #101
Atlanta, GA 30306
(404) 968-2777
newrealmbrewing.com
Recipe by: Grant MacPherson
Dorito-Crusted Scotch Eggs with Cumin-Fennel Marmalade and Pickled Fennel Fronds, Page 120

Cosmic Eye Brewing
6800 P St #300
Lincoln, NE 68505
(531) 500-2739
www.cosmiceye.beer/
Recipe by: Michael Vandenberg
Spicy Shrimp Cocktail, Page 123

Stone Cow Brewery
500 West St B
Barre, MA 01005
(978) 257-8600
www.stonecowbrewery.com
Recipe by: Molly Stevens DuBois
Air-Fried Chicken Wings with Honey Barbecue Sauce, Page 124

The Starkeller
2215 N Garden St
New Ulm, MN 56073
(507) 359-7827
www.schellsbrewery
.combrewery/starkeller
Recipe by: Jace Marti
Mushroom Pasta, Page 126

Resident Culture Brewing Co.
2101 Central Ave
Charlotte, NC 28205
(704) 333-1862
residentculturebrewing.com
Recipe by: Joe Kindred
Grilled North Carolina Grouper with
Pistachio Romesco, Sugar Snap
Peas, and Salsa Verde, Page 128

Crane Brewing Co.
6515 Railroad St
Raytown, MO 64133
(816) 743-4132
www.cranebrewing.com
Recipe by: Chad Tillman
Pan-Seared Halibut with Gose Butter
Sauce and Roasted Vegetables,
Page 131

Von Ebert Brewing
131 NW 13th Ave
Portland, OR 97209
(503) 820-7721
www.vonebertbrewing.com
Recipe by: Dominick Iaderaia
Smoked Adobo Chicken, Page 132
Ensalada de Casa with Cilantro Lime
Vinaigrette and Peach Pico de Gallo,
Page 133

Chapter Seven

Cape May Brewing Co.
1288 Hornet Rd
Cape May, NJ 08204
(609) 849-9933
www.capemaybrewery.com
Recipe by: John Paul Thomas
Waffles with Beer-Berry Compote,
Page 143

Bend Brewing Company.
1019 NW Brooks St
Bend, OR 97701
(541) 383-1599
www.bendbrewingco.com
Recipe by: Zack Beckwith
Grilled Shishito Peppers with Lime
and Salt, Page 144

Two Roads Brewing Co.
1700 Stratford Ave
Stratford, CT 06615
(203) 335-2010
tworoadsbrewing.com
Recipe by: Ryan Keelan
Grilled Pumpkin Flatbread with
Homemade Ricotta and Hot Honey,
Page 146

Dust Bowl Brewing Company
3000 Fulkerth Rd
Turlock, CA 95380
(209) 250-2043
dustbowlbrewing.com
Recipe by: Jesica Lee
Bierocks with Peppered Beef,
Grilled Onions, and Shredded
Cheese, Page 148

Perennial Artisan Ales
8125 Michigan Ave
St. Louis, MO 63111
(314) 631-7300
www.perennialbeer.com
Recipe by: Kevin Willmann
Smoked Chicken Salad, Page 150

Fermentery Form
1700 Palethorp St
Philadelphia, PA 19122
www.fermenteryform.com
Recipe by: Will Lindsay
Falafel and Spiced Yogurt, Page 152

American Solera Brewery
1702 E 6th St
Tulsa, OK 74104
(918) 949-4318
www.americansolera.com
Recipe by: Bic Nguyen
Spicy Caramel Pork with Egg and
Jasmine Rice, Page 155

Carton Brewing Company
6 E Washington Ave
Atlantic Highlands, NJ 07716
(732) 654-2337
cartonbrewing.com
Recipe by: James Avery
Beef Cheek Pie with Stilton Blue
Cheese, Page 156

Chapter Eight

Trillium Brewing
100 Royall St
Canton, MA 02021
(781) 562-0073
www.trilliumbrewing.com
Recipe by: Thomas Park
Johnnycakes with Jonah Crab,
Page 162

Jester King Brewery
13187 Fitzhugh Rd
Austin, TX 78736
(512) 661-8736
jesterkingbrewery.com
Recipe by: Mason Huffman
Kale Caesar Salad with Miso and
Shrimp, Page 165

**Beachwood BBQ +
Brewing + Blendery**
210 E 3rd St
Long Beach, CA 90802
(562) 436-4020
beachwoodbrewing.com
Recipe by: Brian Reese
Braised Pork Belly, Page 166

Revolution Brewing
2323 N Milwaukee Ave
Chicago, IL 60647
(773) 227-2739
www.revbrew.com
Recipe by: Steve Kowaleski
Grilled Cauliflower Steaks with
Butternut Squash Purée, Page 168

Fernson Brewing Company
1400 E Robur Dr
Sioux Falls, SD 57104
(605) 789-3822
www.fernson.com
Recipe by: Ryan Tracy
Zeppole, Page 171

Russian River Brewing Company
725 4th St
Santa Rosa, CA 95404
(707) 545-2337
www.russianriverbrewing.com
Recipe by: Vinnie Cilurzo
Porter Ice Cream, Page 174

Chapter Nine

Frog Alley Brewing Co.
108 State St
Schenectady, NY 12305
(518) 631-4800
www.frogalleybrewing.com
Recipes by: Rich Michaels
Garlic Cheese Spread and Porter
Mustard, Page 181

Athletic Brewing Co.
350 Long Beach Blvd
Stratford, CT 06615
(843) 507-4783
athleticbrewing.com
Recipe by: John Walker
Mango and Beet Salad, Page 185

Pure Project
9030 Kenamar Dr #308
San Diego, CA 92121
(858) 252-6143
www.purebrewing.org/
Recipe by: MIHO
San Diego, California
Lonzino and Aged Gouda Salad,
Page 186

St. Elmo Brewing Co.
440 E St. Elmo Rd G-2
Austin, TX 78745
(737) 300-1965
www.stelmobrewing.com
Recipe by: Tim Bullock
Louisiana Shrimp and Sausage Stew,
Page 189

Switchback Brewing Co.
160 Flynn Ave
Burlington, VT 05401
(802) 651-4114
www.switchbackvt.com
Recipe by: Dan Miele
Maple Sweet-and-Sour Meatballs,
Page 190

Guinness Open Gate Brewery
5001 Washington Blvd
Halethorpe, MD 21227
(443) 575-6893
www.guinnessbrewerybaltimore
.com
Recipe by: Kevin McCarthy
Crab Tortellini with Roast Chard,
Page 192

Community Beer Works
520 7th St
Buffalo, NY 14201
(716) 388-2664
www.communitybeerworks.com
Recipe by: Joe Creegan
Beer Tempura with Pale Ale Dipping
Sauce, Page 194

Sketchbook Brewing Co.
821 Chicago Ave
Evanston, IL 60202
(847) 584-2337
www.sketchbookbrewing.com
Recipe by: John Chiakulas
Peanut Butter Bonbons, Page 196

GLOSSARY

abv—The measurement of alcohol in a beer. The lower the number, the less alcohol is present in the drink.

ale—A beer brewed with *Saccharomyces cerevisiae*, a top-fermenting yeast. Often more fruity and earthy than lagers.

barleywine—A robust ale that is usually high in alcohol content and can have flavors of toffee, plum, fig, cocoa, and more. Drink with caution or risk a tough hangover.

bottle share—A gathering of beer enthusiasts to taste different beers, typically served in small pours.

Brettanomyces—A naturally occurring wild yeast that can impart a peppery, funky, leather, tobacco, or farmyard aroma and flavor to beer.

cold filtered—Primarily a marketing term. Most beer is cold filtered, meaning that it is put through a filter after it's fermented and before it's packaged.

contract brewery or brand—A brewery or brand that uses another facility to make beer. Sometimes this is to meet production demand; other times, this is because the company does not want to focus on operating a brewhouse.

crystal malt—A traditional brewing grain that brings a light color and sweetness to a beer.

Dunkel—A dark lager.

esters—Aromas that are perceivable in beer. Often these mimic familiar fruits.

foeder—A large wooden tank used for aging beer, which often can impart aromas and flavors of the wood into the finished beer.

Gose—A low-abv ale that is identifiable by its slightly salty character.

grain bill—Also known as a malt bill, the combination of grains used in beer recipes. Different styles require different malts at different ratios. A well-constructed grain bill helps define a beer.

hazy—A word used to describe the current IPA trends. Many New England–style beers are unfiltered and contain hops or yeast particles that make them appear hazy.

hops—Small strobiles that grow vertically on bines, or long stems. These perennials require a specific environment to grow cones; they thrive between the 50th and 40th parallels but can grow as low as the 30th parallel (in both hemispheres). Hops add bitterness, aroma, and flavor to beer.

imperial stout—A strong, high-abv dark ale.

IPA—The India pale ale continues to evolve as a beer style. It is the best-selling craft category, with many different varieties on the market. If you see these three letters together, assume that the beer will be hoppy. An imperial, or double, IPA is often stronger in flavor and alcohol.

juicy—A word used to describe the newer generation of India pale ales. It usually indicates that a beer is packed with pounds of hops that impart flavors of juice such as orange, pineapple, mango, and more.

Lactobacillus—A yeast that produces lactic acid rather than alcohol. A popular addition to sour ales.

lager—A beer brewed with *Saccharomyces pastorianus*, a bottom-fermenting yeast that often leaves beers crisp and refreshing.

lambic—A Belgian-style ale produced through spontaneous fermentation. A blend of lambics that are one to three years old is called gueuze.

milk stout—A dark ale brewed with milk sugar for a creamy, sweet texture and flavor.

mixed fermentation—A beer that is the end product of using traditional beer yeast along with wild ale yeasts.

New England–style IPA—A modern take on the traditional India pale ale. Often hazy, with vibrant hop aroma and low bitterness.

pastry stout—A sweet stout that often uses adjuncts to mimic dessert offerings. From bananas and coconut to chocolate and vanilla, these are usually big, boozy, sugar-heavy, decadent ales.

pilsner—A type of lager that is generally crisp, refreshing, and easy drinking.

saison—Also called a farmhouse ale. Traditionally Belgian style, it is brewed with wheat and sometimes lightly spiced.

shandy—Also known as a radler, the combination of a beer with a nonalcoholic beverage, often lemonade or citrus soda, to create a low-abv, refreshing drink.

sour ale—A catchall term for a beer that has a puckering or sour quality, which can come from lactic or citric acids. Sometimes these beers are called wild or spontaneous.

spontaneous fermentation—The act of allowing ambient yeast to inoculate wort to begin fermentation. Often done when wort from the brew kettle is cooled in the open air in a vessel known as a coolship.

stout—Generally a dark beer that mimics flavors of coffee or chocolate. Sometimes served on nitro (think Guinness), giving it a creamy mouthfeel.

two-row barley—A popular grain for brewing that has two rows of seeds on each side of the head. When processed, it is known as two-row malt.

viscous—Thick and tongue coating. Some stouts that are heavy on sugar and alcohol seem as thick as oil, giving a robust impression on the palate.

West Coast IPA—An IPA that is often copper in color and clear, with a pronounced hop bite that some consider bitter. A classic style of beer.

witbier—A white ale brewed with wheat that is often accented with spices such as coriander or citrus. Refreshing and easy drinking.

zymurgy—The study of fermentation.

INDEX

Note: Page references in *italics* indicate recipe photographs.